CW00751330

The Book of the
RALEIGH MOPEDS
All Models

R. H. Warring

ANNOUNCEMENT

By special arrangement with the original publishers of this book, Sir Isaac Pitman & Son, Ltd., of London, England, we have secured the exclusive publishing rights for this book, as well as all others in THE MOTORCYCLIST'S LIBRARY.

Included in THE MOTORCYCLIST'S LIBRARY are complete instruction manuals covering the care and operation of respective motorcycles and engines; valuable data on speed tuning, and thrilling accounts of motorcycle race events. See listing of available titles elsewhere in this edition.

We consider it a privilege to be able to offer so many fine titles to our customers.

FLOYD CLYMER
Publisher of Books Pertaining to Automobiles and Motorcycles

2125 W. PICO ST.   **LOS ANGELES 6, CALIF.**

INTRODUCTION

Welcome to the world of digital publishing ~ the book you now hold in your hand, while unchanged from the original edition, was printed using the latest state of the art digital technology. The advent of print-on-demand has forever changed the publishing process, never has information been so accessible and it is our hope that this book serves your informational needs for years to come. If this is your first exposure to digital publishing, we hope that you are pleased with the results. Many more titles of interest to the classic automobile and motorcycle enthusiast, collector and restorer are available via our website at www.VelocePress.com. We hope that you find this title as interesting as we do.

NOTE FROM THE PUBLISHER

The information presented is true and complete to the best of our knowledge. All recommendations are made without any guarantees on the part of the author or the publisher, who also disclaim all liability incurred with the use of this information.

TRADEMARKS

We recognize that some words, model names and designations, for example, mentioned herein are the property of the trademark holder. We use them for identification purposes only. This is not an official publication.

INFORMATION ON THE USE OF THIS PUBLICATION

This manual is an invaluable resource for the classic motorcycle enthusiast and a "must have" for owners interested in performing their own maintenance. However, in today's information age we are constantly subject to changes in common practice, new technology, availability of improved materials and increased awareness of chemical toxicity. As such, it is advised that the user consult with an experienced professional prior to undertaking any procedure described herein. While every care has been taken to ensure correctness of information, it is obviously not possible to guarantee complete freedom from errors or omissions or to accept liability arising from such errors or omissions. Therefore, any individual that uses the information contained within, or elects to perform or participate in do-it-yourself repairs or modifications acknowledges that there is a risk factor involved and that the publisher or its associates cannot be held responsible for personal injury or property damage resulting from the use of the information or the outcome of such procedures.

WARNING!

One final word of advice, this publication is intended to be used as a reference guide, and when in doubt the reader should consult with a qualified technician.

Preface

THE moped is a class of two-wheeler intermediate between the pedal bicycle and the scooter. It is a considerable step-up from the ordinary bicycle because its 50 c.c. engine is capable of delivering nearly two horsepower; it is also lighter, easier to manhandle and more economical to run than the scooter. The moped also has the efficiency and reliability of a machine designed throughout for a specific duty, and is not just a bicycle to which an engine has been added, as was the case with the earlier power-assisted bicycles.

Like the scooter, the moped first became popular in Continental Europe as a cheap form of personal transport. Raleigh mopeds are based on the best of Continental ideas developed over years of experience in the moped field, allied with traditional Raleigh engineering skill and extensive experience in designing and making two-wheeled vehicles. Spares and Service for these mopeds are readily available in most parts of the United Kingdom.

This handbook includes many technical details of all the Raleigh moped models produced during 1960–69, but *its primary aim is to help moped owners to keep their mounts in sound mechanical condition so as to maintain good performance and reduce depreciation.*

Comprehensive and practical advice on routine and more elaborate maintenance (based on the author's and the maker's experience) forms the main contents of this handbook. None of the maintenance and overhaul work referred to should be beyond the capacity of the average Raleigh moped owner, and a high degree of technical knowledge is not necessary in dealing with a two-wheeler of far less complicated design than a scooter or motor-cycle. An elaborately equipped workshop, garage or lock-up is also not necessary for normal moped maintenance work.

The author sincerely thanks Raleigh Industries Limited of Lenton Boulevard, Nottingham, England, for their generous help to him during the compiling of this maintenance handbook; the instructions included about major overhaul, etc., are largely based on the maker's specific recommendations or instructions. Furthermore, the practical usefulness of this handbook has been considerably enhanced by the makers' according the author permission to reproduce various excellent Raleigh copyright drawings showing detailed exploded views of dismantled moped units. These illustrations, studied in conjunction with the appropriate keys to the numbered parts, should be of considerable assistance to Raleigh moped owners who wish to undertake personally most or all maintenance and overhaul work. It is hoped also that the text in Chapters 3 to 9 will help you to keep your moped in first class condition and thereby obtain maximum satisfaction from it at minimum expense.

OLD BOSHAM, SUSSEX.   R. H. W.

Contents

1 The Raleigh Mopeds

DESIGNED to incorporate the best and most up-to-date Continental technical developments, the first two Raleigh mopeds were introduced towards the end of 1960 and named the "Automatic" Model RM.4 and the "Supermatic" Model RM.5.

Models RM.4 and RM.5. Both these models have a basically similar engine but Model RM.4 is a single-seater machine with an automatic centrifugally-operated clutch and a single speed, and Model RM.5 is a *two-seater* model with an automatic clutch and variable pulley arrangement for automatic gear changing.

The compression ratio on Model RM.5 is 9 to 1 instead of 6·5 to 1 as on Model RM.4; this increase in compression ratio increases the maximum power available to 2·66 B.H.P. at 5,600 r.p.m. compared with 1·7 B.H.P. at 4,500 r.p.m. or 1·39 B.H.P. at 4,000 r.p.m. in the case of the earlier (1960–3) type Model RM.4.

External differences between Models RM.4 and RM.5 are in respect of their styling (*see* Figs. 1 and 2), the fully enclosed chain drive used on Model RM.5, and the different size tyres fitted. During production some minor modifications have from time to time been introduced. Maintenance and overhaul instructions for both models are the same, except as regards a few specific points referred to in this handbook.

Model RM.6. In 1963 the "Runabout" Model RM.6 was introduced. This machine (*see* Fig. 3), while retaining an engine and general specification similar to those of Model RM.4, has had the styling considerably revised; for instance, the fuel tank is behind the saddle and over the rear wheel; the height of the headlamp is raised and bicycle-type front forks are used instead of the telescopic type; the front wheel is also of the bicycle type, and a caliper-operated front brake actuates on the wheel rim.

A *de luxe* version of the RM.6 was launched in September, 1965, but the specification was further improved and the model reannounced as the RM.6 Runabout Super de Luxe on 1st January, 1966. Basically this is simply a comprehensively equipped and finished version of the RM.6, including styled legshields, electric horn and light alloy inflator as standard fittings. Otherwise the specification is identical to that of the RM.6.

Model RM.8. The above-mentioned change in the styling of Model RM.6 is partly embodied in the "Automatic Mk. II" Model RM.8 (*see* Fig. 4) which was introduced in 1964 and superseded Model RM.4. In this

1

case, however, the change in styling includes a reversion to the use of telescopic-type front forks and the inclusion of a hub-type brake for the front wheel.

Model RM.9. In 1964 the single-seater "Ultramatic" Model RM.9 (*see* Fig. 5) appeared. It has styling similar to that used for Model RM.8 and the automatic clutch and variable pulley arrangement provided on Model RM.5 for automatic gear changing; its engine has a compression ratio of 7·5 to 1.

Model RM.12. This model was introduced in 1965 as the "Super 50" RM.12 (*see* Fig. 6). It features the automatic variable-gear transmission, the high performance (9 to 1 compression ratio) engine of the RM.5, and a further change in styling with dropped handlebars and a windscreen to suit the semi-prone position. Basically it is similar to the RM.5, but a single-seater and slightly improved performance.

Model RM.11. This version appeared after the RM.12 but is basically the same machine fitted with upright handlebars, single seat and carrier as a "touring" version.

Model RM.11 "Super Tourist." This version was introduced on January 1st, 1966 and again is similar in basic specification to the RM.12 with 2·66 brake horsepower engine and automatic variable gear transmission. It also has a front mounted fuel tank.

Model "Ultramatic Plus I." This appeared in late 1966/early 1967, being virtually identical to the RM.9 Ultramatic but with a dual seat. One additional model, the Raleigh "Wisp" appeared in May, 1967 and was characterized by having small (12 inch) wheels. Engine and mechanical details remained the same as the RM.6. The production of Raleigh mopeds ceased officially in October, 1969.

SPECIFICATION ("AUTOMATIC" MODEL RM.4)

The specification of Model RM.4 (a single-seater) is briefly as follows—

ENGINE

Type: Single-cylinder two-stroke type with twin transfer ports. Aluminium-alloy cylinder with hard-chrome plated bore. Aluminium-alloy cylinder head and piston. Two cast-iron piston rings.
Bore: 39 mm.
Stroke: 41·75 mm.
Cubic capacity: 49·9 cc.
Piston clearance (bottom of skirt): 0·0004 in. min., 0·0008 in. max.
Piston ring gap: 0·004 in. min., 0·008 in. max.
Crankshaft end float: 0·004 in. min., 0·008 in. max.

IGNITION AND LIGHTING

NOVI flywheel magneto-generator with external H.T. ignition coil.
Contact-breaker gap: 0·016 in.–0·018 in.

Ignition timing: on early engines up to late 1963, $\frac{7}{64}$ in. (0·109 in.)
± 0·004 in. before T.D.C.; on later engines (Frame No. 4R.18102
onwards), $\frac{5}{64}$ in. (0·076 in.) before T.D.C.
Sparking plug recommended: Lodge HN, Champion L86 or KLG F75.
Sparking plug electrode gap: 0·016 in.–0·018 in.
Alternator: NOVI, 18 watt.

CLUTCH

Automatic, centrifugally operated.

PRIMARY DRIVE

Type: Vee-belt.
Ratio: 3·76 to 1.

FINAL DRIVE

Type: roller chain.
Ratio: 3·67 to 1 (12t to 44t).
Chain size: $\frac{1}{2}$ in. × $\frac{3}{16}$ in. × 0·305 in. roller × 96 pitches.

OVERALL GEAR RATIO

13·8 to 1.

FIG. 1. THE MODEL RM.4 "AUTOMATIC"

PEDAL DRIVE

Type: roller chain.
Ratio: 1·78 to 1 (32t to 18t).
Chain size: $\frac{1}{2}$ in. × $\frac{1}{8}$ in. × 0·305 in. roller × 93 pitches.

LAMPS

Headlamp: Luxor.
Headlamp bulb: 6 volt, 15 watt.
Rear lamp bulb: 6 volt, 3 watt.

FUEL SYSTEM

Tank capacity: 1¼ gal.
Carburettor: Gurtner (type BA.10).
Main jet size: No. 20.

TYRES

Size (front and rear): 23 in. × 2 in.
Pressures (lb per sq in.): front, 24; rear, 38.

FRAME NO. POSITION

L.H. frame lug above rear wheel spindle nut.

ENGINE NO. POSITION

Lower front of cylinder barrel

SPECIFICATION ("SUPERMATIC" MODEL RM.5)

Model RM.5 (a two-seater) has a specification which is briefly as follows—

ENGINE

Type: Single-cylinder two-stroke type with twin transfer ports. Aluminium alloy cylinder with hard-chrome plated bore. Aluminium alloy cylinder head and piston. Cast-iron piston rings.
Bore: 39 mm.
Stroke: 41·75 mm.
Cubic capacity: 49·9 c.c.
Compression ratio: 9 to 1.
Maximum B.H.P.: 2·66 at 5,600 r.p.m.
Piston clearance (bottom of skirt): 0·0004 in. min. 0·0008 in. max.
Piston ring gap: 0·004 in. min. 0·008 in. max.
Small-end needle-roller bearing size: 16 mm. O.D., 13 mm. I.D., 14 mm. L.
Crankshaft main bearings size: 42 mm. O.D., 16 mm. I.D., 13 mm. W.
Crankshaft end-float: 0·004 in. min. 0·008 in. max.

IGNITION AND LIGHTING

NOV1 flywheel magneto-generator with external H.T. ignition coil.
Contact-breaker points gap: 0·016 in.-0·018 in.
Ignition timing: $\frac{1}{16}$ in. ± 0·004 in.) before T.D.C.
Sparking plug recommended: Lodge 2HN, Champion L86 or KLG F80.
Sparking plug electrode gap: 0·016 in.-0·018 in.
Alternator: NOV1, 18 watt.

CLUTCH

Type: automatic, centrifugally operated.

PRIMARY DRIVE

Type: Vee-belt.
Ratio: variable (2·78–4·98 to 1).

DIMENSIONS

Overall length: 5 ft. 10 in.
Overall height: 3 ft. 3 in.
Overall width: 1 ft. 11 in.
Weight: 112 lb.

FIG. 2. THE MODEL RM.5 "SUPERMATIC"
The only two-seater in the Raleigh moped range.

FINAL DRIVE

Type: enclosed roller chain.
Ratio: 4 to 1 (48t to 12t).
Chain size: $\frac{1}{2}$ in. × $\frac{7}{16}$ in. × 0·305 in. roller × 103 pitches.

OVERALL GEAR RATIO

11·1–19·9 to 1.

PEDAL DRIVE

Type: roller chain.
Ratio: 1·78 to 1 (32t to 18t).
Chain size: $\frac{1}{2}$ in. × $\frac{1}{8}$ in. × 0·305 in. roller × 93 pitches.

LAMPS

Headlamp: Luxor (rectangular lens).
Headlamp bulb: 6 volt, 15 watt, S.C.C.
Rear lamp bulb: 6 volt, 3 watt, M.E.S.

FUEL SYSTEM

Tank capacity: $1\frac{1}{8}$ gal. (inc. reserve).
Carburettor: Gurtner (type H.14 569 F).
Main jet size: No. 25.

TYRES

Size (front and rear): $22\frac{1}{2}$ in. $\times$ $2\frac{1}{4}$ in.
Pressures (lb. per sq. in.): solo (front), 22; solo (rear), 31; pillion
(front), 23; pillion (rear), 56.

BRAKES

Type: cable operated, internal expanding.
Drum diameter: 100 mm.

FRAME NO. POSITION

Frame steering head.

ENGINE NO. POSITION

Lower front of cylinder barrel.

SPECIFICATION ("RUNABOUT" MODEL RM.6 AND "RUNABOUT DE LUXE")

The specification of Model RM.6 (a single-seater) is briefly as follows—

ENGINE

Type: a 49·9 c.c. single-cylinder two-stroke power unit of the same
type as fitted to the Model RM.4. For details *see* page 2.

IGNITION AND LIGHTING

NOVI flywheel magneto-generator, with external H.T. ignition coil.
Other ignition coil lighting details for Model RM.4 (*see* page 2).
The circuit ignition timing, however, is $\frac{7}{64}$ in. before T.D.C.

CLUTCH

Type: automatic, centrifugally operated.

PRIMARY DRIVE

Type: Vee-belt.
Ratio: 3·76 to 1.

FINAL DRIVE

Type: roller chain.
Ratio: 3·67 to 1 (44t to 12t).
Chain size: $\frac{1}{2}$ in. $\times$ $\frac{3}{16}$ in. $\times$ 305 in. roller $\times$ 96 pitches.

PEDAL DRIVE

Type: roller chain.
Ratio: 1·78 to 1 (32t to 18t).
Chain size: $\frac{1}{2}$ in. × $\frac{1}{8}$ in. × 0·0305 in. roller × 93 pitches.

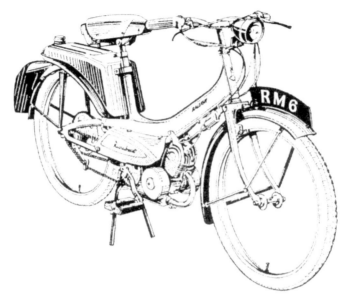

FIG. 3. THE MODEL RM.6 "RUNABOUT"

OVERALL GEAR RATIO

13·8 to 1.

FUEL SYSTEM

Fuel tank capacity: $1\frac{3}{8}$ galls.
Carburettor: Gurtner (type BA.10. 540D).
Main jet size: No. 20.

LAMPS

Headlamp: Sturmey Archer.
  Headlamp bulb: 6 volt, 15 watt, S.C.C.
  Rear lamp bulb: 6 volt, 3 watt, S.C.C.

TYRES

Size (front and rear): 23 in. × 2 in.
Tyre pressure (lb per sq. in.): Front, 24 in.; rear 38 in.

FRAME NO. POSITION

Located in L.H. frame lug above rear wheel spindle nut.

ENGINE NO. POSITION

Located on lower front of cylinder barrel.

SPECIFICATION ("AUTOMATIC MK. 11" MODEL RM.8)

The general specification of the single-seater Model RM.8 is briefly as follows—

ENGINE

Type: single cylinder, two-stroke with twin transfer ports. Aluminium alloy cylinder with hard-chrome plated bore. Aluminium alloy cylinder head and piston. Two cast-iron piston rings.
Bore: 39 mm.
Stroke: 41·75 mm.
Cubic capacity: 49·9 c.c.
Piston clearance (bottom of skirt): 0·0004 in. min., 0·0008 in. max.
Piston ring gap: 0·004 in. min., 0·008 in. max.
Crankshaft end float: 0·004 in. min., 0·008 in. max.

FIG. 4. THE MODEL RM.8 "AUTOMATIC MK. 11"
This model superseded Model RM.4 in 1964.

IGNITION AND LIGHTING

NOVI flywheel magneto-generator with external H.T. ignition coil.
Contact-breaker gap: 0·016 in.-0·018 in.
Ignition timing: $\frac{5}{64}$ in. (0·076 in.) before T.D.C.
Sparking plug recommended: Lodge HN, Champion L86 or KLG F75.
Sparking plug electrode gap: 0·016 in.-0·018 in.
Alternator: NOVI, 18 watt.

CLUTCH

Type: automatic, centrifugally operated.

PRIMARY DRIVE

Type: Vee-belt.
Ratio: 3·76 to 1.

FINAL DRIVE

Type: roller chain.
Ratio: 3·67 to 1 (12t to 44t).
Chain size: $\frac{1}{2}$ in. $\times$ $\frac{3}{16}$ in. $\times$ 0·305 in. roller $\times$ 96 pitches.

OVERALL GEAR RATIO

13·8 to 1.

PEDAL DRIVE

Type: roller chain.
Ratio: 1·78 to 1 (32t to 18t).
Chain size: $\frac{1}{2}$ in. $\times$ $\frac{1}{8}$ in. $\times$ 0·305 in. roller $\times$ 93 pitches.

LAMPS

Headlamp: Wipac.
Headlamp bulb: for a Lucas headlamp, 6 volt, 15/15 watt long-pin bulb is required. For a Wipac headlamp a 6 volt, 15/15 watt offset-pin bulb is necessary.
Rear lamp bulb: 6 volt, 3 watt.

FUEL SYSTEM

Tank capacity: $1\frac{3}{8}$ gal.
Carburettor make: Gurtner (type BA.10).
Main jet size: No. 20.

TYRES

Size (front and rear): 23 in. $\times$ 2 in.
Pressures (lb per sq. in.): Front, 24; rear, 38.

FRAME NO. POSITION

Located on L.H. frame lug above rear wheel spindle nut.

ENGINE NO. POSITION

Located on lower front of cylinder barrel.

SPECIFICATION ("ULTRAMATIC" MODEL RM.9)

Model RM.9 (a single-seater model) has a specification which is briefly as follows—

ENGINE

Type: a 49·9 c.c. single-cylinder two-stroke engine of the same type as that fitted to Model RM.8. For specification details *see* page 8.

IGNITION AND LIGHTING

All specification data given on page 8 for Model RM.8 apply to Model RM.9.

CLUTCH

Type: automatic, centrifugally operated.

PRIMARY DRIVE

Type: Vee-belt.
Variable Ratio: 2·412 to 3·818 to 1.

FIG. 5. THE MODEL RM.9 "ULTRAMATIC"

FINAL DRIVE

Type: roller chain.
Ratio: 4·909 to 1 (54t to 11t).
Chain size: $\frac{1}{2}$ in. × $\frac{3}{16}$ in. × 0·305 in. roller × 101 pitches.

PEDAL DRIVE

Type: roller chain.
Ratio: 1·78 to 1 (32t to 18t).
Chain size: $\frac{1}{2}$ in. × $\frac{1}{8}$ in. × 0·305 in. roller × 93 pitches.

OVERALL GEAR RATIO

11·839 to 18·740 to 1.

LAMPS

The Lucas and Wipac bulb type required are the same as for Model RM.8 (*see* page 9).

FUEL SYSTEM

Fuel tank capacity: 1⅜ gal.
Carburettor: Gurtner (type BA.549).
Main jet size: No. 20.

TYRES

Size (front and rear): 23 in. × 2 in.
Tyre pressures: front, 25 lb per sq in.; rear, 40 lb per sq in.

FRAME NO. POSITION

This is located on the L.H. frame lug above the rear wheel spindle nut.

ENGINE NO. POSITION

This is located low down on the front of the cylinder barrel.

MODEL RM.11, "SUPER TOURIST" AND MODEL RM.17 ("SUPER 50")

The single-cylinder Model RM.12 has the following general specification—

ENGINE

Type: single-cylinder, two-stroke with twin transfer ports. Aluminium alloy cylinder with hard-chrome plated bore. Aluminium alloy cylinder head and piston. Cast-iron piston rings.

Bore: 39 mm.
Stroke: 41·75 mm.
Cubic capacity: 49·9 c.c.
Compression ratio: 9 to 1.
Maximum B.H.P.: 2·66 at 5,600 r.p.m.
Piston clearance bottom of skirt: 0·0004 in. min., 0·0008 in. max.
Piston ring gap: 0·004 in. min.; 0·008 in. max.
Small-end needle-roller bearing size: 16 mm O.D.; 13 mm I.D.; 14 mm L.
Crankshaft main bearings size: 42 mm O.D.; 16 mm I.D.; 13 mm W.
Crankshaft end float: 0·004 in. min.; 0·008 in. max.

IGNITION AND LIGHTING

NOVI: flywheel magneto-generator with external H.T. ignition coil.
Contact-breaker gap: 0·016 in.–0·018 in.
Ignition timing: $\frac{1}{16}$ in. (0·063 in. ± 0·004 in.) before T.D.C.
Sparking plug recommended: Lodge 2HN, Champion L86 or KLG F80.
Sparking plug electrode gap: 0·014 in.–0·016 in.
Alternator: NOVI, 18 watt.

FIG. 6. THE MODEL RM.12 "SUPER 50"

CLUTCH

Type: automatic, centrifugally operated.

PRIMARY DRIVE

Type: Vee-belt.
Ratio: variable (2·78–4·98 to 1).

DIMENSIONS

Overall length: 5 ft 10 in.
Overall height: 2 ft 11 in.
Overall width: 1 ft 10½ in.
Weight: 102 lb.

FINAL DRIVE

Type: roller chain.
Ratio: 4 to 1 (44t to 11t).
Chain size: ½ in. × $\frac{3}{16}$ in. × 0·305 in. roller × 95 pitches.

OVERALL GEAR RATIO

11·1–19·9 to 1.

PEDAL DRIVE

Type: roller chain.
Ratio: 1·78 to 1 (35t to 18t).
Chain size: ½ in. × ⅛ in. × 0·305 in. roller × 93 pitches.

LAMPS

Luxor (round lens).
Headlamp diameter: 4·0 in.
Headlamp bulb: 6 volt, 15 watt, S.C.C.
Rear lamp bulb: 6 volt, 3 watt, M.E.S.

FUEL SYSTEM

Tank capacity: 1½ gal (Imp.) (inc. reserve).
Carburettor: Gurtner (type H.14).
Main jet size: No. 25.

TYRES

Size (front and rear): 23 in. × 2 in.
Tyre pressures (minimum): front, 24 lb per sq in.; rear, 41 lb per sq in.,
The above pressures are based on a rider's weight of 140 lb. For every
14 lb increase in a rider's weight, the front tyre pressure should be
raised by 1 lb per sq in. and the rear tyre pressure raised by 2 lb per sq in.

BRAKES

Type: cable operated, internal expanding.
Drum diameter: front, 90 mm; rear, 100 mm.

FRAME NUMBER POSITION

L.H. frame lug above rear wheel spindle nut.

ENGINE NUMBER POSITION

Lower front of cylinder barrel.

2 Handling your Moped

ALL the Raleigh two-stroke models are true mopeds because they can be pedalled like ordinary bicycles with the engine disconnected from the transmission, or driven as engine-powered bicycles. In the latter case the pedals may still be used, if necessary, to assist the machine, such as when starting from rest or when climbing a steep hill. Pedalling is the normal method of starting.

Riding With and Without Engine Power. For operating your machine purely as a pedal bicycle with the engine disengaged, a special control is

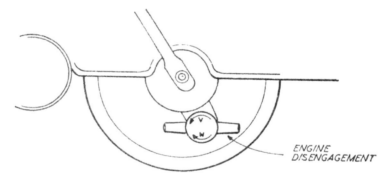

FIG. 7. THE WING-BUTTON CONTROL FOR ENGAGING AND DISENGAGING THE ENGINE

Turning the button *clockwise* engages the engine with the transmission, and turning it *anti-clockwise* disengages the engine. Note that proper engagement is often assisted by rocking the moped slightly backwards and forwards.

provided on the bottom bracket pulley; it comprises a large wing button as shown in Fig. 7. Turning this button as far as it will go in an *anti-clockwise* direction (indicated *V*) disconnects the engine from the drive. Turning the button fully in a *clockwise* direction (indicated *W*) reconnects the engine to the transmission.

With the engine connected as just described, but not actually running, it is still separated from the final drive by the automatic clutch, and the machine can be pedalled at low speeds without the engine being turned over. At a speed of about 4 m.p.h., however, the automatic clutch comes into operation and begins to rotate the engine. This is the normal procedure used for starting, described on page 17.

14

Some Legal Points. Whether ridden with or without the engine connected, the moped is officially classified as a *powered vehicle* and the rider must hold a current "provisional" or "full" *driving licence* covering Group 12 vehicles and be covered by *third-party insurance* as required by the Road Traffic Act. A moped owner must also have and mount on his machine a *registration licence*. If he has never held a "full" (three year) driving licence but only a "provisional" type (valid for six months but renewable), "L" plates must be mounted at the front and rear of the machine.

Note that a moped owner who holds a current "full" driving licence which is endorsed for vehicle categories other than Group 12 must obtain a "provisional" licence for Group 12 vehicles, but need not display "L" plates on his machine.

THE MOPED CONTROLS

Anyone who can ride a bicycle should have no difficulty in riding a Raleigh moped, particularly as no gear changing is involved and the clutch is entirely automatic. All the controls (*see* Figs. 8–10) are mounted on the handlebars and with two exceptions are similar to those provided on an ordinary bicycle.

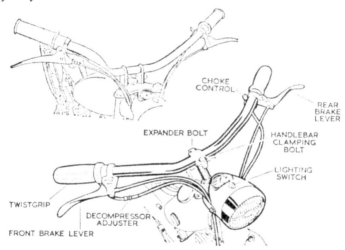

FIG. 8. THE HANDLEBARS AND CONTROL LAYOUT ON
MODELS RM.4 AND RM.5
The inset above shows the layout on earlier type Models RM.4 and
RM.5 (*see* also Fig. 33).

The Choke Lever. The choke control is a small lever mounted underneath the near-side of the handlebars close to the grip. This lever should be used only for adjusting the air-petrol mixture for *starting a cold engine*. A rich mixture is then required. Always close the choke as soon as a cold engine starts and *never use it to start a warm engine*.

The Brakes. The front brake is operated by a lever mounted in front of the handlebar off-side grip, and the rear brake is operated by a lever in front of the near-side grip.

The Combined Throttle and Decompressor Controls. The throttle control is the off-side rubber handlebar-grip, which can be rotated.

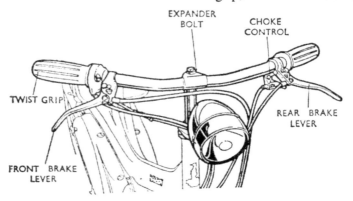

FIG. 9. THE HANDLEBARS AND CONTROL LAYOUT ON
MODELS RM.6, RM.8 AND RM.9

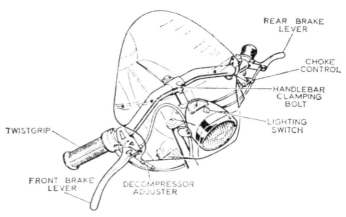

FIG. 10. THE HANDLEBARS AND CONTROL LAYOUT ON
MODEL RM.12

Rotation of this twist-grip *clockwise* (away from the rider) progressively closes the throttle and finally opens the decompressor valve. Twist-grip rotation *anti-clockwise* (towards the rider) at first closes the decompressor valve and then progressively opens the throttle, thereby increasing engine speed and power output. Between the fully open and closed positions of the twist-grip there is a "neutral" position which enables the engine to run at proper tick-over speed, neither too fast nor too slow.

The Lighting Switch. This is mounted on the headlamp and is turned to the "ON" position (*see* page 88) by giving it a quarter of a turn from the "OFF" (fore and aft) position. The electric horn (where fitted) is wired *via* one terminal on the lighting switch and is operated by a separate press-button which can be fitted anywhere on the handlebars.

The Fuel Tap. This is fitted immediately under the fuel (petroil) tank. It has three positions; when turned *downwards* so that it is vertical and in line with the fuel pipe, it is in the "ON" position; when turned *horizontal* it is, according to whether it faces the front or rear, in the "OFF"

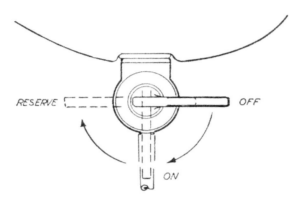

RESERVE   OFF

ON

FIG. 11. SHOWING THE THREE ALTERNATIVE POSITIONS OF THE FUEL TAP

The tap is located at the bottom corner of the fuel tank.

or "RESERVE" position respectively. This is made clear by reference to Fig. 11.

Normally the fuel tap should always be kept in the "ON" position while riding, but turning it to the "RESERVE" position enables a small amount of reserve fuel to be drawn from the bottom of the tank in an emergency. When parking the machine for long or short periods always turn the fuel tap to the "OFF" position.

STARTING AND RIDING

The engine of all Raleigh mopeds is of the two-stroke type which runs on petroil, a mixture comprising petrol and oil, the latter providing all the lubrication necessary for the complete engine unit. It is essential always to use the correct petroil mixture, the correct starting and riding technique and to ride with care and consideration for other road users.

The Petroil Mixture. The recommended petrol/oil ratio for the mixture varies from 16:1 to 20:1, according to the brand and grade of oil used. The higher ratio (16:1) applies to ordinary SAE 30 oils or self-mixing oils, and the lower ratio (20:1) to two-stroke oils or pre-mixed fuels. For running-in purposes the ratio should be increased slightly by using a 12:1 ratio instead of a 16:1 ratio; or a 16:1 ratio instead of a 20:1 ratio.

For convenience of reference, the maker's recommendations for petroil mixtures to use for running-in and normal riding are summarized in Tables I and II. Seven proprietary oils are mentioned. Two-stroke or self-mixing oils should always be used in preference to ordinary engine oils which contain additives which are not necessary with two-stroke engines and in some cases may produce poor running.

"Regular" grade petrols with an octane rating of around 90 are generally quite suitable, although with the higher compression ratio engine (9 to 1) there may be some advantage in running on "Premium" or "Mixture." "Premium" petrols normally have an octane rating of 97–98; "Mixtures" have a slightly lower rating. No advantage is obtained and unnecessary expense is incurred by running on "Super" petrols with an octane rating of 100–102.

Mixing the Petrol and Oil. Ideally, petrol and oil should be mixed in the right proportions in a separate container *before* being put into the tank since the shape of the tank makes it difficult to get good mixing if petrol and oil are added separately to the tank. However, the following procedure is generally satisfactory for "tank mixing"—

1. Turn the fuel tap to the "OFF" position.

2. Add the required amount of petrol to the tank.

3. Add the correct proportion of oil slowly, and simultaneously, to assist mixing of the oil, rock the machine as far as possible without spilling fuel.

4. Replace the fuel tank filler cap and rock or shake the machine to complete mixing of the oil with the petrol.

Starting Procedure. The normal method of starting is to turn on the fuel tap, mount the machine and pedal away. On reaching about 4 m.p.h. (i.e. normal walking speed) and before the engine is felt to "drag" turn the twist-grip *clockwise* to operate the decompressor and, if the engine is cold, also operate the choke control lever. The automatic clutch will come into operation at about this speed, causing the engine to start turning over. The twist-grip can then be rotated anti-clockwise to open the throttle, when the engine should fire and start running. Pedalling can cease as soon as the engine is running and pulling evenly. The choke should be released as soon as possible and in warm weather should not be needed at all for starting. Prolonged use of the choke will only cause the engine to become flooded with petroil and eventually stop.

It will be appreciated that the above technique is equivalent to "push starting," the "push" in this case being provided by pedalling. Also there is no clutch to let in once a certain speed has been built up with the engine "in gear." The engine is always "in gear," but its connection to the transmission is controlled by an automatic clutch.

TABLE I OILS AND PRE-MIXED PETROILS RECOMMENDED FOR RUNNING-IN
(All Raleigh Moped Engines)

Brand	B.P.	Castrol	Esso	Mobiloil	National Benzole	Duckham's	Shell
Oils (two-stroke)	Two-stroke	Two-stroke self-mixing	2T Motor oil	Mobilmix T.T.		Two-stroke oil	2T Motor oil
Petrol/oil ratio	16:1	12:1	12:1	12:1		20:1	20:1
Petroils	"Zoom"	—	—	—	Hi-Fli	—	2T Mixture
Petrol/oil ratio	16:1	—	—	—	16:1	—	20:1

TABLE II OILS AND PRE-MIXED PETROILS RECOMMENDED FOR NORMAL RUNNING
(All Raleigh Moped Engines)

Brand	B.P.	Castrol	Esso	Mobiloil	National Benzole	Duckham's	Shell
Oils (two-stroke)	Energol (two-stroke)	Two-stroke self-mixing	2T Motor oil	Mobiloil T.T.		Two-stroke oil	2T Motor oil
Petrol/oil ratio	20:1	16:1	16:1	16:1		20:1	20:1
Petroils	"Zoom"	—	—	—	Hi-Fli	—	2T Mixture
Petrol/oil ratio	20:1	—	—	—	20:1	—	20:1

Note: On Tables I and II the petrol/oil ratio 20:1 requires ⅘ pint of oil to be added to each gallon of petrol, or 1 pint of oil to 2½ gallons of petrol; the 16:1 ratio requires ½ pint of oil per gallon of petrol; and the 12:1 ratio requires ¾ pint of oil per gallon, or 1 pint of oil per 1½ gallons.

The automatic clutch is really two clutches in one. The *primary* clutch is connected to the engine crankshaft and its operation is governed by *engine* speed. The *secondary* clutch is coupled via the Vee-belt and drive chain to the rear wheel and its operation depends on *road* speed. This secondary clutch comes into operation at a road speed of 4 m.p.h. With the machine at rest and the engine running, the primary clutch disengages at low engine speeds, allowing the engine to "idle." Increasing the engine speed by opening the throttle causes the primary clutch to come into operation and start the machine moving. Once a speed of about 4 m.p.h. has been reached the secondary clutch then comes into effect to lock up the drive and eliminate any slip.

Provided the engine is running, therefore, the machine can be driven away from rest without pedalling, merely by opening up the throttle. Pedal-assisted starting from rest is, however, generally advisable, particularly on a Raleigh moped with fixed ratio transmission; it prevents secondary clutch wear caused by a tendency for some clutch slip to run travelling from rest to about 4 m.p.h.

The engine can also be started with the machine stationary. In this case the machine is raised on to its stand, the twist-grip moved clockwise to operate the decompressor (and the choke lever operated if necessary). One pedal is raised to its highest position and given a smart push forwards. Simultaneously the twist-grip should be rotated anti-clockwise to open the throttle, when the engine should start.

Maintain the throttle slightly open until the engine has warmed up, and then turn the twist-grip clockwise to obtain a good idling position. Apply the rear brake to stop the rear wheel from turning and lower the machine off its stand. It is then ready to mount and ride away, with pedal assistance as necessary. This technique is particularly useful for starting on hills where a "pedal start" would require considerable effort. For all normal starting, however, a "pedal start" should be used.

It must be clearly understood that the stand is designed for supporting the weight of the *machine only*, when the latter is parked, or for engine starting with one foot and the machine stationary; it is not designed to take the additional weight of the rider sitting on the saddle to pedal-start the engine.

Riding Technique. This is essentially similar to that applicable to a bicycle, except that the throttle can be used to impart a certain amount of braking effect, as well as acceleration. To stop, the twist-grip is turned to the "neutral" position and both brakes applied. The most efficient way of braking is to apply the rear brake first, and then the front brake if more braking effort is required. Once the speed falls below 4 m.p.h. the automatic clutch will disengage and the machine will come to a stop with the engine idling.

To stop the engine it is only necessary to operate the decompression by turning the twist-grip clockwise as far as it will go.

With full engine power in use and the machine running normally, pedalling can also be used when more effort is required to prevent the engine from labouring under unfavourable conditions, such as when climbing hills or facing a strong head wind. All Raleigh mopeds should be capable of climbing moderately steep hills under their own power, but if road speed falls below about 8 m.p.h. the engine will start to labour and should be assisted by pedalling.

The need for pedal assistance is less likely on models fitted with automatic variable transmission because this transmission automatically selects the best drive ratio appropriate for the prevailing road conditions. Pedal assistance is therefore only likely to be required when climbing the steepest of hills.

Riding with Maximum Comfort. The saddle and handlebars can be readily adjusted for height on all models, and the handlebars can also be adjusted for rake on some models. Correct adjustments to suit the

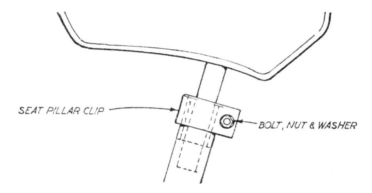

SEAT PILLAR CLIP

BOLT, NUT & WASHER

FIG. 12. THE SIMPLE ADJUSTMENT PROVIDED FOR ALTERING THE SADDLE HEIGHT

On all models it is only necessary to loosen the bolt on the saddle-pillar clip and then slide the saddle pillar up or down as required.

individual rider make for better riding comfort and better control. Basically the aim should be to see that the rider's weight is comfortably "balanced" between the saddle, pedals and handlebars.

The saddle can be adjusted for height by loosening the bolt on the saddle pillar clip (*see* Fig. 12), sliding the saddle pillar to the required height and then retightening the bolt.

Handlebars can be adjusted for height by unscrewing the central expander bolt about three turns. The bolt should then be tapped with a soft hammer or wooden mallet. This will free the internal expander cone and allow the handlebar height to be adjusted. After checking that the handlebars are still at right angles to the front wheel, the expander bolt can then be retightened.

Handlebar height can be adjusted over a fairly wide range, but it is essential that at least $2\frac{1}{2}$ in. of the handlebar stem remains within the steering head, otherwise the handlebars are not securely fastened.

To adjust the handlebar for rake, loosen the handlebar-clamp bolt where applicable (Models RM.4, RM.12), rotate the handlebars to the desired position and retighten the clamp.

TABLE III

RECOMMENDED TYRE PRESSURES*

Moped Model	Front Tyre (lb per sq in.)	Rear Tyre (lb per sq in.)
RM.4	24	38
RM.5 (Solo). . .	22	31
RM.5 (Pillion) . .	23	56
RM.6	24	38
RM.8	24	38
RM.9	25	40
RM.12 . . .	24	41

* The recommended tyre pressures given in Table III are based on the rider's weight being approximately 10 stone. For every increase in weight by one stone the life of the tyres will be considerably lengthened by increasing the front and rear tyre pressures by 1 lb per sq in. and 2 lb per sq in. respectively.

Recommended Tyre Pressures. Maintaining correct tyre pressures is essential both for safe riding and in order to obtain maximum life from the tyres. Pressures cannot be judged with any accuracy by pressing on the tyres and a proprietary pressure gauge such as the Dunlop pencil type No. 6, the Romac, the Schrader No. 7750, or the Holdtite should be used. The recommended tyre pressures for all 1960–66 models are summarized in Table III. Pressures should be checked at frequent intervals. Note the considerable difference in the rear tyre pressure recommended in the case of the two-seater Model RM.5 when ridden solo and when carrying a pillion passenger.

Running-in the Engine. Proper running-in is *absolutely essential* to obtain maximum performance and long life from your two-stroke engine. The running-in period recommended by the makers (for a new machine or one fitted with a new or reconditioned engine) is 300–500 miles. During this vital period the use of petroil mixture with a higher oil content than that used for normal running is advised (*see* Table II). It is also undesirable to exceed the maximum road speeds given in Table IV.

During the running-in period the engine should *never* be allowed to labour, and pedal assistance should *always* be used when riding away from a standing start, or when climbing hills. The engine should also not be "raced" or run at full throttle, although short bursts of full throttle

TABLE IV

RECOMMENDED MAXIMUM RUNNING-IN SPEEDS

Raleigh Moped Type	Maximum Road Speed (First 500 miles)
Model RM.4 . .	25 m.p.h.
Model RM.5 . .	30 m.p.h.
Model RM.6 . .	25 m.p.h.
Model RM.8 . .	25 m.p.h.
Model RM.9 . .	25 m.p.h.
Model RM.12 . .	30 m.p.h.

are beneficial towards the end of the running-in period. The engine should never be allowed to idle longer than is necessary, otherwise it may become overheated and cause piston and possibly other damage of a serious nature.

Regular maintenance (dealt with in Chapter 3) must, of course, be attended to during the running-in period, paying special attention to checking Vee-belt and chain tension. Tension should be checked and if necessary adjusted after riding 100 miles, 300 miles and 500 miles. During running-in check all external nuts and bolts at intervals for tightness, especially those concerned with the engine. Some initial bedding down and slackness invariably occurs during the running-in period.

3 Regular maintenance

BESIDES attending to lubrication and some minor weekly maintenance, less frequent but *regular* attention must be given to certain items which require checking and adjustment if your machine is to be kept in good running order. Regular and correct maintenance not only maintains the good operating efficiency of your machine but, also prolongs its useful life. It also concerns overall economy. Everything that needs to be done within the regular maintenance schedule is well within the capabilities of the average owner.

Lubrication. Engine lubrication is dealt with in Chapter 2 (*see* pages 17–18). The lubrication of the various "bicycle" parts is dealt with at various points in this chapter. It is important to use the right type of lubricants. These comprise three types: a thick oil for chain lubrication; a thinner oil for lubricating the freewheel, control cables, pivots and working joints, etc.; and a single grade of grease for all items which require greasing. The recommended proprietary lubricants are summarized in Table V and these (or their equivalents) should always be used for the oiling and greasing points summarized on page 28 and in Table VI respectively.

Weekly Maintenance. Attend to the following—

1. Check the tyre pressures (*see* page 22), using a proprietary pressure gauge. The pressures should be checked with the tyres *cold* and not immediately after a run when they are often warm and their pressures a little higher than normal. After checking pressures and re-inflating the tyres as necessary, the valve caps must be replaced and screwed up finger-tight. These act as dust covers and protect the cores of the valves. A lost valve cap should be renewed as soon as possible.

At the same time as you are checking the tyre pressures, examine the tyre treads for wear or embedded nails or flints. Such objects must be removed and if a tyre shows obvious signs of damage, such as a deep cut, it should be repaired as soon as possible. Renew any cover which has its tread worn away or seriously damaged.

Tyres should always be kept free from oil or grease and if such lubricants do accidentally get on to the rubber treads they should be cleaned thoroughly with a cloth moistened with petrol. Properly looked after, and always run at the correct inflation pressures, tyres should have a very long life, but the wear rate is also affected by how a moped is ridden. Fierce braking and sharp cornering, for example, considerably increases tyre wear and reduces tyre life.

2. Clean the vehicle with a weak solution of household detergent, applied liberally and lightly, but not rubbed in. All the paintwork and brightwork should then be rinsed or hosed off with a copious supply of clean water before the detergent solution has had a chance to dry. A final sponge over with clean water, followed by leathering to remove any smear marks, should then be adequate. This can be followed by wax polishing or, if preferred, polishing with a car type cleaner-polish or "quick polish."

During washing some water may get into the brake drums, but this is not important although the brakes may be ineffective for a short period when again used. If this is so, applying the brakes while riding will quickly dry out the drums and restore normal braking efficiency. When washing the machine, and particularly if hosing it down, take reasonable care not to wet the brake drum areas unduly, and also avoid allowing water to get in on the ignition coil and electrical system.

3. Check the brake and other handlebar controls for easy and correct operation. If any controls are at all stiff, the pivot points at each end, and the exposed inner ends of all control cables, should be lubricated with *thin* oil. Normally, however, the lubrication of such points is only required at 500 mile or monthly intervals. If a weekly check shows that the brakes are losing their effectiveness, however, they should be re-adjusted (*see* page 33) and not left until the 1,000 mile check is made.

A point which normally requires lubrication at weekly intervals in winter (500 miles in summer) is the nipple on the near-side of the bottom axle-bracket; this should have a little grease (*see* Table V) applied to it with a grease gun. On Model RM.6 oil the front brake caliper pivots weekly.

Other Maintenance. The remainder of routine maintenance should be carried out at regular mileage or monthly intervals as detailed under the sub-headings which follow. Except where a moped is used fairly continuously for very short trips only (thus covering only a small mileage during long periods of use), maintenance should be planned on a *mileage basis*.

Every 500 Miles (or Every Month). The following maintenance is necessary—

1. The tension of both chains (pedal and power-drive) should be checked and if necessary adjusted as described on page 31. When the rear wheel is turned there is one point where the chain is most taut. At this position the chain, if correctly tensioned, should have about ½ in.-¾ in. up-and-down movement at the centre of the chain run when it is moved with the fingers. Note, however, that in the case of Models RM.4, RM.6, RM.8, RM.9 RM.11 and RM.12 chain tension must be checked *with the machine on its stand*; in the case of Model RM.5 only, the chain tension must be checked *with the rider sitting on the machine*.

If your machine is in continuous and extensive daily use it is advisable to check the chain tension *weekly* rather than at 500 mile or monthly intervals.

2. Lubricate the freewheel with *light* oil, using an oil-can. The outside of the freewheel should be cleaned with a cloth moistened with petrol and oil then applied with the oil-can to the gap between the inner and outer

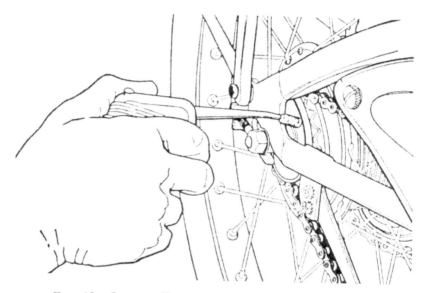

FIG. 13. OIL THE FREEWHEEL ABOUT EVERY 500 MILES
Apply an oil-can as shown between the inner and outer parts of the freewheel.

parts of the freewheel as shown in Fig. 13. At the same time pull the chain backwards to rotate the outer part of the freewheel and assist the oil to penetrate into the freewheel mechanism.

3. Remove and inspect the sparking plug. The gap between the centre and outer electrodes should be 0·016 in.-0·018 in. and the plug should be in good condition. To re-gap the sparking plug after cleaning, use a plug re-gapping tool (obtainable from plug manufacturers or accessory firms); it usually includes suitable feeler gauges for checking the gap. Always bend the *outer* electrode(s) and never the centre electrode.

Quick cleaning of a sparking plug which is in reasonably good condition can be done by brushing its points with a small wire brush and then lightly rubbing some emery cloth on their firing sides. Thorough cleaning of a really dirty plug is best done by handing the plug to a garage for quick cleaning and testing with the modern equipment now usually installed.

4. Clean the carburettor air filter. To do this unclip the air cleaner body or loosen the clamp bolt holding the air cleaner in place and remove it

from the carburettor. Remove the filter gauze and wash both parts in clean petrol. Then dry out and replace.

5. Lubricate all handlebar control-lever pivots, exposed inner portions of all control cables, pedal end-caps, stand pivot and all other pivot points with *thin* oil, using an oil-can. In wet weather lubrication about every 250 miles is desirable.

6. On Models RM.4, RM.8, RM.9, RM.11 and RM.12 apply the grease gun to the two nipples on the telescopic front forks and give *two or three strokes*. Also give *one stroke* to the central nipple on the automatic clutch.

7. On all models apply the grease-gun to the central nipple provided for clutch lubrication.

8. On mopeds with variable-speed drive (Models RM.5, RM.9, RM.11 and RM.12) the clutch and variable-transmission pulley mechanism should be greased through the central grease nipple, and the steel balls well oiled with SAE 50 oil. The mechanism should also be kept clean; if necessary, remove the Vee-belt, press the pulley cheeks together to expose the steel balls and wash the assembly (including the housing) thoroughly with petrol or paraffin. When dry, oil generously with SAE 50 oil.

9. In wet weather it pays to clean the bottom-bracket pulley and chain sprocket and apply a coating of grease to the gap between the sprocket and hub. This will ensure that the sprocket remains free to move relative to the pulley and that the sprocket does not seize.

Every 1,000 Miles (or Every 2 Months). Attend to the 500 miles service dealt with on pages 25–27, and also the following—

1. Remove both chains and clean, lubricate and replace them at the correct tension (*see* pages 31–32).

2. Remove the fuel filter from the carburettor or the filter gauze from the filter chamber (according to the model concerned), wash it in clean petrol and replace. On some models an additional filter is fitted in the fuel pipe-line which can also be readily removed and cleaned by swilling through with petrol.

A fuel filter is also fitted in the fuel tap, but this can only be removed for cleaning by draining the fuel tank, removing the fuel pipe and unscrewing the tap. This is *not* necessary for routine maintenance unless the fuel is known to be dirty or the tank itself has become dirty.

3. On the Models RM.5, RM.11 and RM.12 apply *one stroke* of the grease gun to the nipple provided on the speedometer-drive gearbox.

4. Check and if necessary adjust both brakes (*see* page 33).

Every 3,000 Miles (or Every 6 Months). Attend to the 1,000 mile service just dealt with, and also the following—

1. On models RM.5, RM.11 and RM.12 remove the speedometer drive and grease the inner cable sparingly.

2. Clean out both wheel hubs and re-pack their bearings with fresh grease. At the same time clean and smear grease sparingly on the brake operating cams and spindles. (This does not apply to Model RM.6.)

TABLE V

RECOMMENDED LUBRICANTS (ALL RALEIGH MOPEDS)
(For engine oils and pre-mixed petroils *see* page 19.)

Brand	B.P.	Castrol	Duckham's	Esso	Mobiloil	Shell
Oiling points · ·	Energol SAE 20W	Castrolite	NOL Twenty	20W/30	Mobiloil Artic	X-100 20W
Greasing points · ·	Energrease L2	Castrolease L.M.	L.B.10	Multi-purpose grease H	Mobilgrease M.P.	Retinax A
Chains and pulley balls	Energol SAE 50	Grand Prix	NOL Fifty	40/50	B.B.	X-100 50

TABLE VI

Greasing Points and Mileage Intervals (All Models)
(All oiling points are dealt with in the text on pages 21–23.)

Item on Model	RM.4	RM.5	RM.6	RM.8	RM.9	RM.11 and RM.12
Front forks (two nipples)	500	—	—	500	500	500
Clutch (central nipple)	500	500	500	500	500	500
Variable-transmission pulley (clutch and central nipple) . .	—	500†	—	—	500	500
Speedometer-drive gearbox . . .	—	1,000	—	—	—	1,000
Speedometer-drive cable (smear) . .	—	3,000	—	—	—	3,000
Bottom-bracket pulley bearings (nipple of near-side) .	500*	500*	500*	500*	500*	500*
Wheel hubs (repack)	3,000	3,000	3,000	3,000	3,000	3,000
Brake cams and spindles (smear) . .	3,000	3,000	3,000	3,000	3,000	3,000
Steering head (repack)	12,000	12,000	12,000	12,000	12,000	12,000

* Weekly intervals recommended in winter.
† 1,000 miles in summer.

3. Decarbonize (not the engine) and clean the exhaust system (*see* page 51).

4. Check the condition of the contact-breaker contacts and clean and adjust them as necessary (*see* page 53). The gap between the contacts should be 0·016 in.- 0·018 in.

Every 6,000-8,000 Miles. Full decarbonizing of both the engine and its exhaust system can be expected to be needed every 6,000-8,000 miles, the exact mileage interval depending on how the machine is ridden and maintained. For decarbonizing instructions *see* Chapter 6 (pages 49-51). It is also recommended that a new sparking plug of the recommended type (*see* Specifications in Chapter I) be fitted at this mileage.

About Every 12,000 Miles. At intervals of about 12,000 miles it is recommended that the steering head be dismantled, the bearings cleaned and re-packed with new grease (*see* page 74).

TRANSMISSION, BRAKES, WHEELS

This section contains some useful practical advice about the general maintenance of the above three items.

Removal and Adjustment of Vee-Belt. The Vee-belt for the primary drive is accessible if the near-side fairing and clutch guard are removed (the off-side fairing also in the case of Models RM.4, RM.6 and RM.8).

On Models RM.4, RM.6 and RM.8 the belt is tensioned by *pivoting the engine*. Thus to remove the belt, first slacken the upper and lower engine-attachment bolts. Then pivot the engine *rearwards to its full extent*. The belt can now be removed, taking it off the bottom-bracket pulley first. When replacing the belt, fit it first over the clutch pulley and then over the bottom-bracket pulley.

To increase belt tension on the three above-mentioned models insert a "soft" lever, such as a hammer handle (*see* Fig. 14) between the bottom-bracket housing and the lower-mounting bolt and lever the engine *forward* until the correct belt tension is obtained. The tension is correct when finger pressure applied to the belt midway between the two pulleys produces just a small amount of up-and-down movement.

On Models RM.5, RM.9, RM.11 and RM.12 the Vee-belt is automatically kept in correct tension by a spring and *no adjustment is required*. The belt can be removed by slackening the bolts and pushing the engine back against the tensioner spring, taking the belt off the bottom-bracket pulley first.

Removing and Cleaning Chains. Either chain can be removed by separating its connecting link and pulling the chain off its sprockets. When refitting a chain it is imperative, to prevent its possibly coming adrift, to replace the spring clip on the connecting link so that its *closed end faces the direction of chain movement*.

When a chain is removed it can be cleaned by immersing it in a shallow tray filled with paraffin and scrubbing it clean with a stiff brush. Allow the chain to soak in the paraffin for some time. To re-lubricate the chain stand a tin of SAE 50 oil in a pan of very hot water and lower the chain into the tin. Permit the chain to soak in hot oil for at least 15 minutes. Then withdraw the chain and hang it up long enough to enable all surplus

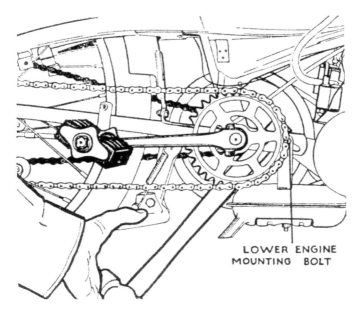

LOWER ENGINE
MOUNTING BOLT

Fig. 14. Adjusting the Tension of the Vee-belt Used
for the Primary Drive

This adjustment applies only to Models RM.4, RM.6 and RM.8.
On the remaining three mopeds the belt is automatically tensioned by
means of a spring.

oil to drain off. Before replacing the chain, clean and lightly oil the chain sprockets.

Chain Wear. This can be checked by laying the chain out on a flat surface and measuring the distance between the centres of 23 links, i.e. 23 pitches. This should be $11\frac{1}{2}$ in. on a new chain, but is naturally increased by wear. When the 23 pitch measurement increases to $11\frac{3}{4}$ in. the chain is *badly* worn and should be renewed.

Chain Tension Adjustment. This is effected with the moped on its stand (all models except Model RM.5) and the rear wheel rotated until the drive chain is in its tightest position. Referring to Fig. 15, loosen both rear wheel spindle nuts and slacken fully the brake-arm wing nut. Also slacken the pedal chain by loosening the two bolts holding the jockey-wheel arm and swinging it out of the way.

With the appropriate spanner turn each drive chain adjuster an *equal*

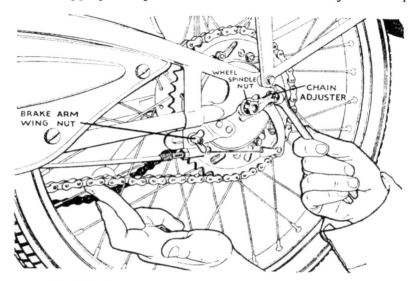

FIG. 15. ADJUSTING THE TENSION OF THE DRIVE CHAIN

The adjustment of the drive chain, which transmits engine power to the rear wheel, is the same on all models, but note that on Model RM.5 the adjustment must be made with your weight on the machine.

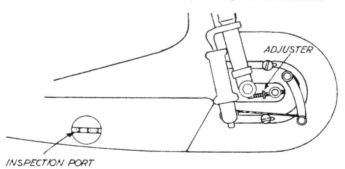

FIG. 16. SHOWING THE DRIVE CHAIN ADJUSTER AND CHAINCASE INSPECTION PORT ON A MODEL RM.5 WITH FULLY ENCLOSED DRIVE CHAIN

The arrangement shown applies to all models having the drive chain fully enclosed in a chaincase.

amount, moving the rear wheel in the slotted chain lug until the chain has ½ in.-¾ in. up-and-down movement at the centre of the run when finger pressure is applied. The wheel spindle nuts can then be firmly tightened; make sure that the rear wheel is in true alignment with the front wheel.

Set the pedal chain to its tightest position and adjust the jockey wheel to produce a similar ($\frac{1}{2}$ in.-$\frac{3}{4}$ in.) vertical whip at the centre of the chain run. On Model RM.5 a "Buret" pedal-chain tensioner has been fitted from June 1965 onwards. This tensioner has the name "Buret" stamped on the tensioner arm for identification. It is an automatic type and requires no adjustment.

Chain tension affects the adjustment of the rear brake, and the brake must be adjusted as necessary after completing adjustment of the chain.

On Model RM.5 the procedure required for drive chain adjustment is the same as for the other models, except that the adjustment must be made with *the rider sitting on the machine*. On models with a fully-enclosed chain a plug must be removed from an inspection port in the centre of the lower part of the chain case; this exposes the centre of the lower chain run as shown in Fig. 16.

Transmission Overhaul. Some useful general advice is given in Chapter 7.

Adjusting the Brakes. Brake adjustment (referred to on page 25) is very simple. The adjusters for both the front and rear brakes are screwed into the handlebar-lever pivots and are easily adjusted without tools.

Adjustment should always be made so that each brake begins to "bite" with a minimum amount of movement of the control lever and without the brake shoes continually binding on the brake drums. After each adjustment is made the machine should be mounted on its stand and the wheel turned to ensure that it spins freely without any binding.

Removing and Fitting Front Wheel. To remove the front wheel (all models except Model RM.6), first slacken off the front brake adjuster and remove the cable from the cam lever. Also disconnect the speedometer cable from the drive unit (where applicable). Then loosen the wheel spindle nuts and disengage the washers from the recesses in the front-fork ends. The wheel can now be withdrawn from the forks.

When refitting the front wheel on all models except Model RM.6, follow the reverse order of removal and note that it is important that the brake-plate peg engages correctly with the slot in the off-side fork end.

Model RM.6 does not have hub brakes and therefore front wheel removal and fitting is simplified. To remove the wheel it is only necessary to slacken off the front brake adjuster sufficiently for the tyre to pass between the brake blocks, loosen the wheel spindle nuts and withdraw the wheel.

When replacing the front wheel of Model RM.6 check that the bearing adjustment is correct, i.e. see that there is only the merest trace of side play when the spindle nuts are tightened up. After fitting the rear wheel it is, of course, necessary to adjust the front brake.

Removing and Fitting Rear Wheel. To remove the rear wheel (Models RM.4, RM.6, RM.8, RM.9, RM.11 and RM.12) first slacken the pedal chain jockey-wheel, remove the brake arm wing nut and bolt, and disconnect the rear brake cable. Then loosen the wheel spindle nuts sufficiently to enable the chain adjusters to be pulled out of the slots in the frame lugs, and push the wheel *forward*. Both chains can now be lifted off their sprockets and the rear wheel withdrawn without having to split the two chains.

In the case of Model RM.5 the rear section of the chain case has first to be removed by unscrewing the two screws holding it to the hub flange and then sliding the chain case rearwards. The pedal chain jockey-wheel can then be sprung out of the way and the wheel spindle nut(s) unscrewed and the spindle pulled out. Both chains can now be pulled off their sprockets without splitting them and the wheel withdrawn from the frame as soon as the brake cable is disconnected.

When replacing the rear wheel follow in reverse the removal procedure, taking care to ensure that the brake plate anchoring slot and the brake outer cable are properly located; also see that the wheel spindle is pushed firmly up against the adjusting screws before tightening the spindle nuts.

4 Fault finding

SHOULD a fault develop, the process of finding the real cause and then putting it right should be tackled systematically. Fortunately the Raleigh moped is a fairly simple machine and faults are most likely to be due to simple causes which can readily be put right rather than serious mechanical failures. The maker's own recommendations on the more likely faults and their causes are extremely comprehensive and are with permission reproduced below. It will be seen that the "cause" is more often than not faulty operation, or produced by lack of attention to regular maintenance.

ENGINE TROUBLE

Engine Will Not Start or Stops of its Own Accord. This may be because of—

(a) **FAULTY CARBURATION.** This may be because of—

1. Absence of fuel: refill the tank.
2. Fuel tap is not turned on: open the tap.
3. Carburettor is loose causing air leak: tighten.
4. Carburettor jet is blocked: remove and clean the jet. At the same time clean the float chamber and filter and blow through the internal passages in the carburettor.
5. Fuel feed line is blocked: clean out fuel pipe, tap and filters, preferably by blowing through with compressed air. Before replacing the pipe on the carburettor connection, turn on the tap to verify that fuel is flowing.
6. Fuel filler-cap air vent is blocked: clear vent.
7. Flooded carburettor: turn off the fuel tap, dry the carburettor by opening the throttle wide and kicking the engine over as rapidly as possible. If it does not fire after a few attempts, dry and clean the sparking plug. Before replacing, turn over the engine several times in order to eject the excess fuel from the cylinder. Then turn on the fuel tap again and carry out normal starting procedure. Should flooding still occur, check the float, float needle and seating.
8. Engine is flooded with fuel due to excessive use of choke control: remedy as in point (7).
9. Choke plunger in carburettor is not returning: check plunger and operating cable and adjust as necessary. Remedy as in point (7).
10. Water in fuel: drain fuel system, clean out carburettor. Refill with correct fuel.

(*b*) **FAULTY IGNITION.** Possible cases are—

11. Dirty or oiled sparking plug: clean the plug (*see* page 26).

12. Sparking plug electrode gap too wide: reset the gap (*see* page 26). If the electrodes are badly burnt or corroded, replace the plug.

13. Faulty or broken sparking plug insulator: replace the plug.

14. Sparking plug lead disconnected: reconnect lead.

15. Insulation of H.T. lead to sparking plug faulty and spark shorting to earth: wrap the lead temporarily with insulating tape and replace it as soon as possible.

16. Dirty or loose connection in the ignition circuit: check all connections and clean or tighten as necessary.

17. Dirty, burnt or maladjusted contact-breaker points: clean or re-face points and set to correct gap (*see* page 53).

18. Condenser or external gap H.T. ignition coil faulty: have them checked.

19. Note: The sparking plug could get "wetted" with fuel due to carburettor flooding or to faulty ignition. It could be fouled by descending a long hill without opening ·the throttle occasionally, or by letting the engine run light for too long. A sparking plug running too hot may cause the engine to stop due to "whiskering," which is the formation of a conducting filament between the electrodes. A sparking plug running too cold fouls easily.

(*c*) **MECHANICAL TROUBLE.** Mechanical trouble may originate through—

20. Leakage at a crankcase joint, or at the crankshaft oil seals. Leakage at cylinder head gasket or at decompressor valve.

If the Engine Starts. but Stops Immediately. Should this occur—

21. In winter with a cold engine: let the engine warm up with the cold start control in operation.

If the Engine. Stops when the Throttle is Open. This may result because—

22. Engine is still cold: allow it to warm up.

23. Carburettor jet is blocked: clean it.

24. Fuel has difficulty in reaching S.U. carburettor: clean the petrol pipe, tap and filters (*see* also points (1), (4), (5) and (6)).

If the Engine Does Not Run Properly or Lacks Power. Potential causes are—

25. Mixture too weak: *see* points (1), (3), (4), (5), (6) and (20). Jet too small: fit one size larger jet.

26. Mixture too rich (air cleaner is blocked with dirt, float does not maintain correct fuel level or jet is loose): wash the air cleaner in petrol or adjust or repair the carburettor as necessary. Jet is too large: fit one size smaller jet.

27. Too much oil in petroil mixture: correct the mixture (*see* page 17).

28. Sparking plug dirty or unsuitable type, or has electrodes corroded or with incorrect gap: clean plug and set gap, or if necessary renew the plug (*see* Specification in Chapter 1).

29. Contact breaker, condenser or ignition coil not functioning properly: have them checked.

30. Exhaust port or exhaust system choked with carbon: decarbonize and thoroughly clean (*see* page 51).

31. Sparking plug loose in head: tighten it securely.

32. Mechanical trouble: *see* points (3) and (20).

33. Piston rings gummed-in or excessively worn: clean grooves. Clean rings or replace if necessary.

If the Engine Four-Strokes Excessively. Possibly this may be because—

34. Mixture is too rich: remedy as indicated in point (26).

35. Exhaust system is choked: remedy as indicated in point (30).

Note: If the four-stroking is caused by too rich a mixture, this can easily be verified by turning off the fuel tap whilst riding the machine. Just before the engine stops due to lack of fuel, it will begin to fire correctly. If this does not prove to be the cause, then it is probably due to carbon deposits obstructing the exhaust system.

Misfiring. Consider these possibilities—

36. Fault with ignition equipment: check all items in equipment.

37. Fuel feed deficiency producing a weak mixture (usually accompanied by spitting-back in the carburettor: *see* points (1), (3), (4), (5) and (6).

If the Engine Stops of its Own Accord. This can be due to—

38. Fuel feed deficiency or absence of fuel if the stoppage is preceded by spitting-back in the carburettor and back-firing in the exhaust.

39. An ignition defect if the stoppage is preceded by a bout of misfiring.

If the Engine Races but the Moped Does Not Increase Speed. Perhaps—

40. The Vee-belt is slipping: check condition of belt and adjust or renew as required. (The belt can be contaminated by grease or oil due to excessive lubrication of the transmission.)

LIGHTING TROUBLE

Failure of Lights (Engine Running). This can be the result of blown bulb(s). Check by substitution of both headlamp and rear lamp bulb together. Otherwise if the headlamp bulb is defective the rear lamp bulb will blow due to overloading.

If after checking the bulbs as described above, the bulbs still do not light with the engine running, proceed to check the generating coil as follows—

1. Connect a test lamp, consisting of a spare headlamp and rear lamp bulb connected in parallel to give an 18-watt load across the main lead from the generator and a convenient point on the engine. With the engine running at a fast tick-over, the bulbs should light to near full brilliancy.

2. If, after carrying out the test described in (1) the test bulbs light, proceed to check each stage of the circuit from the generator to the lighting switch, referring to a wiring diagram (if available) for open-circuits (breakages, etc.). Should any of these faults exist, the bulb will not light. Also check for bad connections, etc., if the bulbs light dimly.

Light Flicker (Engine Running). Examine the wiring for loose or dirty connections, or short circuits caused by faulty cable insulation. Check the bulb contacts. Rectify as necessary.

Headlamp Illumination Insufficient. Check for discoloured bulbs or sagged filaments; replace the bulbs if necessary. Check the reflector; if tarnished or discoloured it should be renewed, as aluminized reflectors should not be cleaned or polished in any way whatsoever.

MISCELLANEOUS TROUBLE

Certain faults other than those already dealt with may develop and may be of more obscure origin, or require more elaborate treatment. The advice given in this section is based on the main troubles which service agents, etc., have experienced since the introduction of the first Raleigh Mopeds. More detailed maintenance is described in other chapters.

Lack of Power and Drive Slip. By far the most common cause of lack of power is drive slip and the Vee-belt should be checked regularly for wear and freedom from grease, and for correct tension (Models RM.4, RM.6 and RM.8 only). Belt tension and adjustment are dealt with on page 30. The loss of power due to a slipping belt is most noticeable when climbing hills or riding on full throttle at speeds above 15 m.p.h.; it is further aggravated by wet road conditions.

A slipping clutch can also be a cause of lack of power. This can occur on new or relatively new machines through excessive lubrication which causes the clutch linings to become contaminated with grease. The only cure in such cases is to remove the clutch drum and wash off the clutch linings thoroughly with petrol or a similar solvent.

Clutch slip can, of course, also take place when the clutch linings become badly worn. In this case the linings must be renewed.

The effect of a slipping clutch (particularly if due to over-greasing) is most noticeable by the lack of power and poor acceleration which occur when moving away from a standing start.

Carbon deposits accumulating in the exhaust pipe and silencer can also cause loss of power. As it is a simple matter to remove and dismantle the silencer and exhaust pipe assembly for examination, this cause should be suspected first when loss of power occurs and the machine has covered 2,500-3,000 miles or more.

Slipping ignition timing is also a cause of loss of power. The symptoms in this case are usually that the engine drives the rear wheel with the machine mounted on its stand but lacks power to pull the machine away from a standing start with the rider in position.

Slipping timing occurred on earlier models because the specified tightening torque for the nut holding the flywheel in position was insufficient. This tightening torque has now been increased to 36 lb/ft. It is important to appreciate that this applies only to new machines, or when fitting a new cam, as this relatively high torque allows for the initial stretch or "creep" of new components. When re-assembling or re-fitting a used cam a tightening torque of 30 lb/ft should not be exceeded on the flywheel nut.

Rear Chain Adjustments. On a number of "Automatic" Model RM.8 mopeds damage has occurred to the bottom-bracket pulley due to its coming into contact with the drive chain. The cause has invariably been due to lack of proper maintenance, i.e. failure to check and re-adjust the chain tension periodically (*see* page 31). A guide plate is fitted to prevent the chain from contacting the pulley, but this is not effective if the chain becomes excessively slack or the guide plate is bent out of position. Normally, with the chain correctly tensioned, there should be about $\frac{1}{8}$ in. clearance between the guide plate and the chain.

Sprocket Seizure. This can be caused by the ingress of moisture and dirt causing seizure between the bottom-bracket pulley and the chain sprocket, with the result that the drive cannot be disengaged. If this occurs the sprocket should be freed from the pulley and the hub, and the interior of the sprocket cleaned and then polished with an abrasive cleaner (or fine emery cloth). The hub should be smeared with molybdenum disulphide grease before refitting the sprocket and a coating of grease applied to the gap between the sprocket and hub after fitting.

The Pedal Chain Tensioner. If the pedal chain tensioner is bent or otherwise damaged there is the possibility that the pedal chain may jam in the guide piece which surrounds the tensioner wheel when the machine is pedalled. This can cause further damage to the tensioner, and possibly even to the rear wheel spokes. Therefore should there be the slightest hint of the pedals jamming, immediately check that the bottom run of the pedal chain is directly in line with the top run. If it is not, the tensioner is bent or displaced and needs immediate attention.

From July 1965 onwards an improved type of pedal-chain tensioner has been fitted to Model RM.5; it can be identified by the name "Huret" stamped on it. This new tensioner is interchangeable with the original one (unmarked), but component parts of the two different types are not interchangeable.

Speedometer Cable Breakage. This is almost invariably caused by bad positioning of the speedometer cable which, if detached for any reason, should always be replaced to provide the best possible run without any sharp bends. On Model RM.5 the speedometer cable should leave its drive box approximately parallel with the front swinging-arm.

"Squealing" Brakes. This can occur through a variety of causes, and sometimes is even associated with changes in atmospheric conditions. The following is recommended by Raleigh Industries Limited as the correct procedure to deal with "squealing" brakes—

1. Thoroughly clean the wheel hubs and roughen the brake linings.
2. Chamfer the leading edge of each brake lining slightly.
3. Check the wheel bearings for adjustment or wear.
4. Check the tension of the wheel spokes.
5. When reassembling the hub, make certain that the brake backplate is firmly locked.

5 Carburettor and fuel system

ALL Raleigh mopeds are fitted with Gurtner carburettors, three types of which are used (*see* Table VII). The BA.10 and H.14 types are illustrated in considerable detail in Figs. 17 and 18 respectively. The general notes and maintenance instructions in this chapter apply to *all* carburettors fitted to 1960–6 Raleigh mopeds.

TABLE VII

GURTNER CARBURETTORS FITTED TO 1960–6 MODELS

Moped Model	Carburettor Type	Main Jet Size
RM.4 . .	BA.10 54OD	No. 20
RM.5 . .	H.14 569F	No. 25
RM.6 . .	BA.10 54OD	No. 20
RM.8 . .	BA.10 54OD	No. 20
RM.9 . .	BA.549	No. 20
RM.12 . .	H.14 569	No. 25

The Throttle-stop Screw. The only adjustment on the Gurtner carburettor is the throttle-stop screw which controls the maximum closing of the throttle slide and thus the "tick-over" or idling speed. Normally this is adjusted until the engine idles smoothly and at a reasonably low speed without hesitating or stopping. Screwing in this screw (clockwise) increases the idling speed; unscrewing the speed decreases the idling speed.

The Main Jet. During normal running the mixture is controlled by the fixed main jet. The size of the jet fitted to each new machine has been carefully chosen to give optimum performance with the recommended fuel (petroil) mixture over the widest possible range of use. It is possible to adjust the mixture for normal running by replacing the standard size main jet with one of slightly different size (*see* Table VIII). Note that a lower size No. represents a smaller diameter jet giving a weaker mixture; a higher No. indicates a larger diameter jet giving a richer mixture. It is unlikely that an alteration in main jet size will prove beneficial except when riding in unusual conditions such as extremely hot or cold weather. In the United Kingdom extreme weather conditions rarely prevail. The average moped owner is recommended *not* to experiment with different

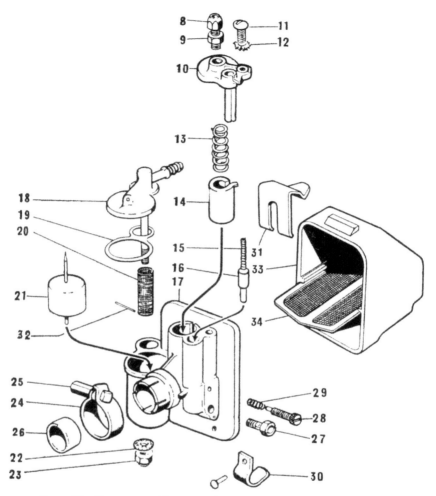

FIG. 17. EXPLODED VIEW OF GURTNER TYPE BA AND BA10
CARBURETTOR FITTED TO MODELS RM.4, RM.6, RM.8
AND RM.9

8. Throttle cable adjuster	22. Fibre washer
9. Lock-nut for 8	23. Cap nut
10. Mixing chamber cover	24. Carburettor attachment clip
11. Securing screw for 10	25. Bolt and nut for 24
12. Washer for 11	26. Insulating sleeve
13. Return spring for 14	27. Main jet
14. Throttle slide	28. Throttle-stop screw (adjustable)
15. Return spring for 16	29. Locking spring for 28
16. Choke plunger	30. Lower clip for air cleaner
17. Carburettor body	31. Upper clip for air cleaner
18. Float chamber cover	32. Pin for 31
19. Joint washer for 18	33. Air cleaner body
20. Fuel filter gauze	34. Air cleaner gauze
21. Float	

TABLE VIII

ALTERNATIVE MAIN JET SIZES FOR GURTNER CARBURETTORS

Raleigh Moped Model	Standard Jet Size	Size for Weaker Mixture	Size for Richer Mixture
RM.4 . . .	20	19 or 18	20·5 or 21
RM.5 . . .	25	24	26
RM.6 . . .	20	19 or 18	20·5 or 21
RM.8 . . .	20	19 or 18	20·5 or 21
RM.9 . . .	20	19 or 18	20·5 or 21
RM.12 . . .	25	24	26

main jet sizes. Where running trouble or loss of performance directly attributable to an incorrect mixture occurs, the cause is more likely to be some other fault (*see* page 35), such as a sticking or damaged carburettor float or an air leak, rather than an unsuitable size main jet.

Removing Carburettor from Cylinder Barrel. For the carburettor to be accessible the engine fairings must be removed. Before attempting to remove the carburettor make sure that the fuel tap is turned off. Pull off the fuel line (on Models RM.4, RM.6, RM.8 and RM.9), or unscrew the cap-nut on top of the float chamber and take off the banjo union (on Models RM.5 and RM.12). The carburettor attachment clip can then be loosened and the carburettor tilted towards the near-side. This gives access to the top of the mixing chamber so that its securing screw can be removed and the cover lifted off, together with the throttle valve and spring and the choke. The remainder of the carburettor can then be removed for further dismantling if required.

Dismantling and Cleaning Instrument. Remove the air cleaner. Then remove the two screws and spring washers securing the float chamber cover and lift off the cover. This exposes the float and needle assembly which can be withdrawn. Check that the seal which fits under the float-chamber cover is undamaged. Renew it if necessary.

The needle which determines the level of petroil in the float chamber is located in the float by a spring clip which engages one of *three* grooves on the needle. Normally the clip is located in the *bottom* groove which gives the lowest fuel level. The float can be fitted to the needle either way up, but when re-assembling, the point of the needle must be uppermost.

The main jet is screwed into the bottom of the carburettor body and can be readily removed for cleaning. The jet should be rinsed in petrol and its hole blown through or pricked clean with a stiff bristle. Never use a wire for cleaning the main jet as this can enlarge the hole and thereby upset the mixture air/petrol ratio.

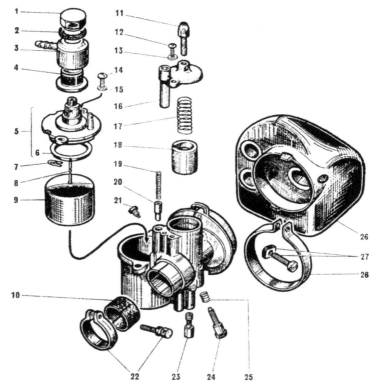

FIG. 18. EXPLODED VIEW OF GURTNER H14 CARBURETTOR
FITTED TO MODELS RM.5 AND RM.12

Note that on earlier type RM.5 models the design of the float chamber
and air cleaner was somewhat different to the later design illustrated.
Parts for the earlier and later designs are not interchangeable.

1. Banjo union cap-nut
2. Fibre washer for 1
3. Banjo union
4. Filter
5. Float chamber cover assembly
6. Sealing ring for 5
7. Clip for 8
8. Float chamber needle
9. Float
10. Fibre sleeve
11. Throttle cable adjuster
12. Mixing-chamber cover screw
13. Washer for 12
14. Screw for 5

15. Washer for 14
16. Mixing chamber cover
17. Return spring for 18
18. Throttle slide
19. Return spring for 20
20. Choke plunger
21. Throttle slide guide-screw
22. Carburettor attachment clip
23. Main jet (No. 24)
24. Throttle-stop screw (adjustable)
25. Locking spring for 24
26. Air cleaner
27. Screw and nut for tightening or
loosening 28

28. Air cleaner attachment clip

After dismantling the carburettor all parts should be washed in clean petrol and left to dry, or if possible blown dry with compressed air. When the float-chamber cover is refitted check that the point of the needle is correctly located in its seat and that the cover is properly secured. Also see that the main jet is screwed home tight. When attending to cleaning do not neglect to screw out the throttle-stop screw and clean it thoroughly; also clean all interior passages in the carburettor by flushing them through

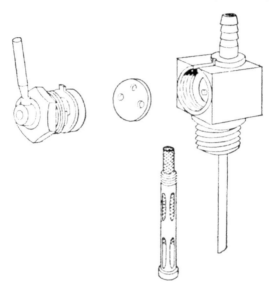

FIG. 19. DISMANTLED FUEL TAP (EARLIER MODELS)

with petrol and then blowing compressed air through them, e.g. using a bicycle pump.

The Throttle and Choke Cables. If necessary the throttle valve can be detached from its cable by compressing the valve spring until the cable nipple (*see* Fig. 35) can be withdrawn from its recess. The choke valve can be detached by loosening the clamp screw at the handlebar end so that the operating lever has approximately $\frac{1}{16}$ in. free play. Adjustment of the throttle cable should be made, when necessary, with the cable adjuster located on top of the carburettor mixing chamber. This adjuster can be manipulated with an 8 mm spanner and should be set so that there is always a slight amount of free play in the cable when the twist-grip is in the "neutral" position used for slow-running.

The Fuel Tap. The fuel tap fitted in the bottom of the tank can be removed by unscrewing it after draining the tank. It is only necessary to remove this tap for cleaning the internal gauze filter, or for changing the petroil seal.

Fuel taps differ in external appearance and design on different models (*see* Figs. 19 and 20), but all types can be dismantled for renewing the petroil seal by removing the gland nut of the tap. The old seal must be removed by lifting it out with the point of a knife blade or a similar tool. The tap should be cleaned before a new seal is fitted, and care must be

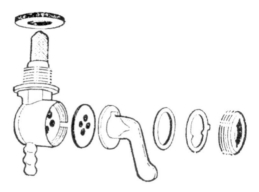

FIG. 20. DISMANTLED FUEL TAP (LATER MODELS)

taken to locate the seal correctly on the three spigots inside the tap. Also before re-fitting and tightening the gland nut, examine the seating face of the valve for burrs or damage, and make good as necessary. When ordering spare parts state the name ("Orlandi" or "Karco") of the tap marked on it. A tap bearing the latter name is fitted to the tank of all later models.

6 Overhauling power unit

THE power unit comprises: the engine, the flywheel magneto-generator, the automatic clutch and the exhaust system. The instructions given in this chapter apply specifically to Models RM.8 and RM.9, but are generally applicable to *all* 1960-6 models although there are some slight detail differences. These will generally be obvious and the detailed exploded views of the engines installed on Models TM.8 and RM.5, RM.12, shown in Figs. 21 and 22 respectively, are a useful guide in this respect.

Some 1963-5 Modifications. In 1963 the power output of the "Automatic" Model RM.4 engine was increased from 1·39 b.h.p. to 1·7 b.h.p., the chief modifications being a new cylinder head and cylinder barrel (with matched piston), and connecting-rod and crankshaft assemblies as specified on Model RM.5. The modified engine was fitted to all RM.4 models from Frame No. 4R.18102 onwards, and to all 1964 and later RM.8 models.

A modification introduced in July 1965 and affecting all Model RM.4 and RM.5 machines was an increase in the diameter of the clutch and magneto retaining threads on the crankshaft from 10 mm to 11 mm. This affects the size of the flywheel retaining nut (Part No. MMN228 now MMN227) and the clutch-drum nut should renewal be required. Note that crankshaft assemblies ordered as spare parts are supplied complete with their retaining nuts.

DECARBONIZING

As mentioned on page 30, this is usually required every 8,000–10,000 miles.

Preliminary Dismantling (All Models). To gain access to the engine the knurled screws holding the fairings in place must be unscrewed and the fairings then detached. Disconnect and remove the sparking plug lead and also the L.T. wire from the other end of the ignition coil. This wire must be threaded back through its retaining bracket to clear the frame. Then detach the lighting wire which is clipped to the terminal behind the magneto stator-plate.

Detach the decompressor cable. To do this, depress the decompressor valve on the cylinder head and remove the inner cable from the loop in the end of the valve spring. The cable nipple can then be unhooked from its stop plate on the cylinder head.

Disconnect the fuel feed-pipe from the Gurtner carburettor (after first

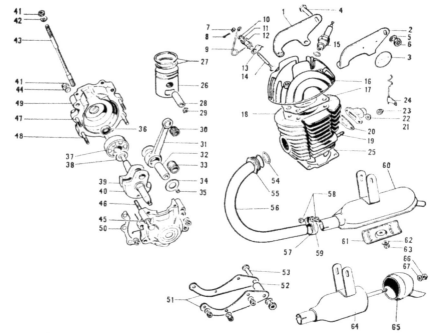

FIG. 21. EXPLODED VIEW OF POWER UNIT, EXHAUST SYSTEM, ETC., OF MODEL RM.8

1. Engine mounting bracket (R.H. upper)
2. Engine mounting bracket (L.H. upper)
3. Engine No. plate (self-adhesive)
4. Bolt (upper engine mounting)
5. Shake-proof washer for 4
6. Nut for 4
7. Decompressor-valve yoke
8. Decompressor-valve pin
9. Hairpin spring for decompressor valve
10. Retaining washer for 11
11. Decompressor valve seal
12. Decompressor valve body
13. Anchor plate for decompressor cable
14. Decompressor valve
15. Sparking plug
16. Cylinder head
17. Cylinder head gasket
18. Cylinder barrel
19. Stud for inlet flange
20. Inlet-flange joint washer
21. Inlet adaptor
22. Shake-proof washer for 19
23. Self-locking nut for 19
24. L.T. cable retainer
25. Gasket for base of cylinder barre
26. Piston
27. Piston rings (two)
28. Gudgeon-pin
29. Circlip (one of two) for 26
30. Small-end needle-roller bearing
31. Connecting-rod assembly
32. Crankpin
33. Big-end needle-roller bearing
34. Crankpin washer
35. Taper plug for end of crankpin
36. Crankshaft oil seal
37. Ball journal bearing for crankshaft
38. Shim washer for crankshaft (0·1, 0·2, or 0·3 mm thick)
39. Crankshaft half (magneto side)
40. Crankshaft half (clutch side)
41. Nut for 43
42. Spring washer for 43
43. Crankcase stud for securing cylinder barrel and head
44. Shake-proof washer for crankcase bolt 46
45. Plain washer
46. Crankcase bolt (7 × 1·25 × 45 mm)
47. Crankcase bolt (7 × 1 × 30 mm)
48. Crankcase bolt (7 × 1 × 47 mm)
49. Crankcase half (off-side)
50. Joint washer for crankcase halves
51. Engine mounting plates (lower)
52. Spacer for 51
53. Bolt and nut (lower engine mounting)
54. Gasket for exhaust pipe flange
55. Nut to secure 56 to cylinder barrel
56. Exhaust pipe
57. Clip securing 56 to silencer
58. Bolt and nut for 57
59. Shake-proof washer for 58
60. Silencer (complete)
61. Silencer access plate
62. Washer for access plate stud
63. Nut for access plate stud
64. Burgess silencer body
65. End cap for 64
66. Lock-nut securing 65 to silencer
67. Plain washer for 66

making sure that the fuel tap is turned off), loosen the carburettor attachment-clip screw and tilt the carburettor towards the near-side of the machine. This enables the screw holding the mixing-chamber cover to be reached and the cover lifted off, together with the throttle and choke valves. The carburettor can then be removed from the cylinder barrel.

To Remove the Engine from the Frame (Models RM.4, RM.6 and RM.8). Attend to preliminary dismantling as just described. Loosen the top and bottom engine-mounting bolts, push the engine to the *rear* as far as it will go, and take the Vee-belt off the bottom-bracket pulley. Now push the engine *forward* until the lower mounting bolt is clear of the pedal chain-wheel; the nut and washer can then be removed and the bottom bolt pulled out.

The exhaust system can now be removed *complete* after unscrewing the large nut securing the exhaust pipe to the cylinder barrel.

To remove the engine from the frame, place a box or other support under the crankcase (or as convenient) and remove the top engine-mounting bolt. The engine can then be eased out.

To remove the Vee-belt, loosen the two bolts holding the belt guard and then remove the belt.

To Remove the Engine from the Frame (Models RM.5, RM.9 and RM.12). First deal with preliminary dismantling as described on page 47. Next remove the clutch guard which is held by three screws. Then push the engine back against the tensioning spring and remove the Vee-belt, taking it off the bottom-bracket pulley first.

The nut and bolt holding the tensioning spring to the bracket on the lower engine-mounting plate should now be removed. Support the engine to prevent it dropping, remove the nut on the upper engine-mounting bolt and withdraw this bolt. The engine can then be removed, complete with the exhaust system.

Decarbonizing the Engine. Removal of the cylinder barrel is *not* necessary unless it is desired to inspect or remove the piston rings, and possibly the piston (*see* page 59–60). With the engine removed from the frame as described above, unscrew the four nuts on the cylinder barrel studs and remove the cylinder head, taking care not to lift the cylinder barrel as well, and so break the joint between the cylinder barrel and crankcase. Hold the cylinder barrel and turn the flywheel until the piston rises to its uppermost (T.D.C.) position. A soft metal scraper can then be carefully used to scrape all carbon deposits from the top of the piston, i.e. its crown. Be very careful not to scratch the piston crown surface, and on no account polish it with an abrasive.

Hold the cylinder barrel again and further rotate the flywheel until the piston descends to its lowest (B.D.C.) position. This exposes the *exhaust port* which should similarly be scraped clean of all carbon deposits, taking care not to scratch the cylinder barrel bore. All traces of carbon should

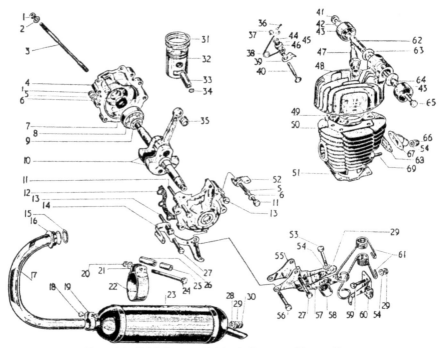

FIG. 22. RM.5 AND RM.12 POWER UNIT, ETC.

1. Nut for 3
2. Shake-proof washer for 3
3. Stud securing cylinder barrel and head
4. Crankcase half (off-side)
5. Spring washer for crankcase bolt 11
6. Plain washer for crankcase bolt 11
7. Crankcase oil seal
8. Crankshaft main bearing
9. Shim washer for crankshaft (0·2, 0·3, or 0·1 mm thick)
10. Crankcase assembly
11. Bolt securing crankcase halves and clutch fairing bracket
12. Joint washer for crankcase halves
13. Bolt securing crankcase halves
14. Bracket for clutch fairing
15. Gasket for exhaust pipe flange
16. Nut to secure 17 to cylinder barrel
17. Exhaust pipe
18. Bolt, washer and nut for 19
19. Clip securing 17 to silencer
20. Nut for 24
21. Shake-proof washer for 24
22. Silencer clip
23. Silencer
24. Bolt for silencer clip 22
25. Spacer for silencer clip (13·2 or 18·3 mm long)
26. Spacer for silencer clip (25 or 33 mm long)
27. Crankcase bolt
28. Plain washer for nut securing silencer end-cap
29. Nut securing silencer end-cap
30. Lock-nut for 29
31. Piston ring (one of two)
32. Piston
33. Gudgeon-pin
34. Circlip (one of two) for 32
35. Small-end needle bearing
36. Decompressor-valve pin
37. Decompressor-valve yoke
38. Decompressor-valve spring
39. Anchor plate for decompressor cable
40. Decompressor valve
41. Nut for upper engine-mounting bolt 65
42. Shake-proof washer for 65
43. Bush for engine-mounting bolt 65
44. Retaining washer for decompressor-valve seal
45. Decompressor-valve seal
46. Decompressor-valve body
47. Sparking plug
48. Cylinder head
49. Cylinder head gasket
50. Cylinder barrel
51. Gasket for base of cylinder barrel
52. Bracket for clutch fairing (upper)
53. Bolt for lower engine mounting
54. Shake-proof washer for 53
55. Engine-mounting bracket (R.H. lower)
56. Crankcase bolt
57. Engine-mounting bracket (L.H. lower)
58. Rubber bush for lower engine mounting
59. Bolt for lower engine-mounting bracket
60. Spring-retaining bracket
61. Springs for tensioning Vee-belt
62. Spacer for upper engine mounting (32 mm long)
63. Plug for upper engine mounting
64. Spacer for upper engine mounting (14 mm long)
65. Bolt for upper engine mounting
66. Self-locking nut for inlet port stud
67. Inlet port adaptor
68. Gasket for inlet port face
69. Stud on inlet port face

then be blown out of the cylinder barrel, using compressed air if possible. A bicycle pump can be used if an air-line is not available.

Before replacing the cylinder head on the cylinder barrel its combustion chamber surface should be scraped thoroughly clean and a new gasket fitted. After replacing the cylinder head fit the four securing nuts and tighten them evenly a little at a time until fully tight. Avoid tightening the nuts excessively.

Decarbonizing the Exhaust System. This does *not* necessitate the removal of the engine from the frame. The complete exhaust system can be detached from the cylinder barrel and frame with the engine in position.

On all models except Model RM.9 unscrew the large nut securing the exhaust pipe to the cylinder barrel and slacken the silencer holding clip. The complete exhaust system can then be removed. The silencer can now be disconnected after removing its retaining nut and washer. Scrape all carbon deposits out of the exhaust pipe and silencer, paying particular attention to cleaning the holes in the silencer inlet and tail pipe baffle.

On Model RM.9 only remove the silencer end-cap and the large nut holding the exhaust pipe to the cylinder barrel. The exhaust pipe, complete with central rod and baffle plates, can then be removed from the silencer body. Clean all internal parts and surfaces thoroughly, scraping off all carbon deposits.

Before re-fitting the exhaust pipe (all models), the *exhaust port* on the cylinder barrel should be scraped thoroughly clean. To enable this to be done, turn the flywheel until the piston is at its lowest (B.D.C.) position, fully opening the exhaust port. When decarbonizing this port take great care not to allow any loose carbon deposits to enter the cylinder bore.

It is advisable to fit a new exhaust port gasket when replacing the exhaust pipe after decarbonizing.

The Decompressor Valve. Should the decompressor valve need attention, follow the dismantling instructions for decarbonizing the engine up to the removal of the cylinder head.

To remove the decompressor valve, first cut off the head of its retaining pin and withdraw the pin, holding the spring so that the assembly cannot fly apart when released. The valve can then be pushed out for examination.

If the valve is burned or pitted it should be ground-in with *fine grade* grinding paste. Check also that the plastic seal in the valve guide is in perfect condition and not causing leakage around the valve stem. Renew the plastic seal if it is in poor condition. Finally, re-assemble the decompressor valve, fitting a new retaining spring.

THE IGNITION SYSTEM

The Magneto-Generator. This is covered by the flywheel. The latter is retained on the crankshaft by a nut with a left-hand thread. To remove, hold the flywheel stationary and unscrew this nut. The flywheel can then be pulled off its register on the cam, the latter remaining on the crankshaft.

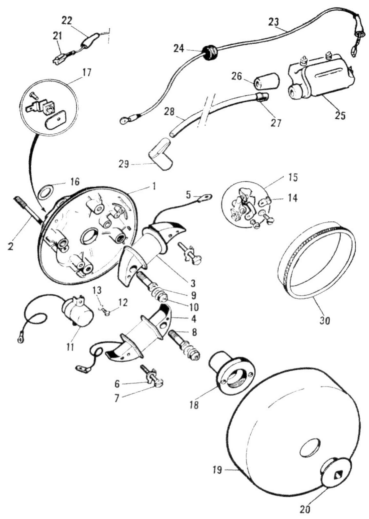

FIG. 23. FLYWHEEL MAGNETO-GENERATOR (ALL MODELS)

1. Stator plate
2. Stud securing 1
3. Lighting coil
4. Ignition coil (L.T.)
5. Terminal tag (internal coils)
6. Tab-washer for ignition coil securing-screw
7. Securing-screws for coils 3 and 4
8. Securing-screws (hollow) for coils 3 and 4
9. Belleville washers for 8
10. Self-locking nuts for 8
11. Condenser
12. Screw securing 11
13. Spring washer for 12
14. Contact-breaker adjusting clip

15. Contact-breaker assembly
16. Sealing ring for stator plate
17. Lighting terminal assembly
18. Cam
19. Magneto flywheel
20. Flywheel retaining nut (11 mm thread)
21. Terminal tag
22. Plastic cover on terminal tag
23. Ignition L.T. lead
24. Grommet on L.T. wire
25. H.T. ignition coil (external)
26. Cap for H.T. lead to coil
27. Terminal of H.T. lead
28. H.T. lead
29. Waterproof cover for sparking plug
30. Coil centralizing ring

Re-fitting is straightforward, except that it is important to ensure that the two pegs on the back of the flywheel locate in the holes in the cam.

The Contact-breaker. Removal of the flywheel (*see* previous paragraph) gives access to the contact-breaker, details of which are shown in Fig. 22. The condition of the points can be checked by rotating the engine until the contacts are fully open. If oily or dirty, clean the contacts with a non-fluffy rag dipped in pure petrol (e.g. lighter fuel) or methylated spirits. If the points are blackened, insert a strip of very fine garnet paper between

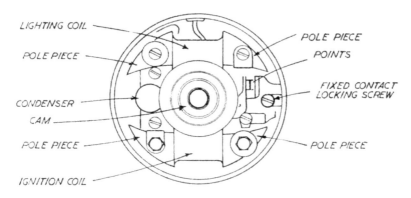

FIG. 24. ARRANGEMENT OF THE CONTACT-BREAKER, IGNITION COIL, LIGHTING COIL, ETC.

them, turn the engine to close the contacts and draw the paper out. Repeat this several times with the abrasive side towards each point in turn. If the points are slightly pitted they can be refaced using a special contact file (*not* an ordinary flat file or any other abrasive). Badly pitted or worn points should be replaced.

To check the contact-breaker gap (every 3,000 miles), after examining the condition of the contacts and if necessary cleaning them, rotate the engine until the contacts are *fully open* and then measure the gap between them with a feeler gauge. This should be 0·016 in.-0·018 in. If the contact-breaker gap is incorrect, loosen the fixed contact locking-screw and move the contact by inserting a screwdriver blade in the slot in the spring clip and twist in the required direction. Tighten the locking-screw after making the adjustment and again check the gap.

If necessary, the contact-breaker can be removed complete by removing the screw and washer and taking off the three leads from the insulated terminal. Then remove the fixed contact locking-screw and the spring clip. The contact-breaker can then be withdrawn.

When replacing, or fitting a new contact-breaker, check that the spindle peg locates in the drilled boss in the stator plate and also that none of the leads are trapped between the contact-breaker and the stator plate.

Sparking Plugs. *See* Specifications in Chapter I and page 26.

The Ignition Coil. *See* page 87.

Ignition Timing. The cam at ignition timings for all models are stated in the Chapter 1 Specifications and in the footnote. Should it be necessary to adjust the timing a special cam extractor and a crankshaft thread protector (*see* Fig. 27) must be used to withdraw the cam, or free it on the crankshaft. To retime the ignition correctly an ignition-advance gauge (*see* Fig. 27) is also required for screwing into the cylinder head in place of the sparking plug.

With the gauge in position and the cam removed, or loose on the crankshaft, rotate the engine until the plunger in the centre of the gauge rises to its highest position (indicating the top-dead-centre position of the piston). Now turn the engine backwards until the piston has fallen by $\frac{5}{64}$ in. (0·076 in.).* Hold the engine in this position and replace the cam in such a position that the contacts of the contact-breaker are just beginning to open. Give the cam a sharp tap with a soft hammer or a wooden mallet to hold it on the crankshaft and refit the flywheel after checking that the contact-breaker gap is correct.

THE AUTOMATIC CLUTCH

An automatic centrifugally-operated type clutch is on all models fitted on a crankshaft taper at the opposite end to the flywheel.

Removal of Clutch Unit (All Models). To remove the clutch drum the flywheel should be held stationary and the central (14 mm) clutch drum-securing nut unscrewed. Unless a box spanner is used, however, the grease nipple in the centre of this nut should first be removed with a 6 mm spanner.

To withdraw the clutch drum a special extractor is required and also a thread protector (*see* Fig. 27) for fitting to the end of the crankshaft. Screw the extractor fully into the hub and then tighten the extractor bolt. If undue resistance is felt, tap the head of the extractor bolt with a hammer while tightening the bolt. When the clutch drum is free the extractor and thread protector can be removed and the drum slid off. The key should also be removed from the shaft and kept in a place where it cannot be lost.

The clutch body is located on the crankshaft by one 22 mm internal circlip and one 15 mm external circlip. Remove in this order: the internal circlip, the shims, the locating washer and the external circlip; then pull the clutch body off the crankshaft, together with another locating washer and the needle-roller bearing which are still in position. These can then be withdrawn.

---

* This timing applies to the Model RM.4 engine *after* frame No. 4R.18102, and all Model RM.8 and RM.9 engines. For Model RM.4 engines (*before* frame No. 4R.18102) and the Model RM.6 engine, the timing dimension before T.D.C. is $\frac{7}{64}$ in. For Model RM.5 and RM.12 engines the timing dimension is $\frac{1}{16}$ in. before T.D.C.

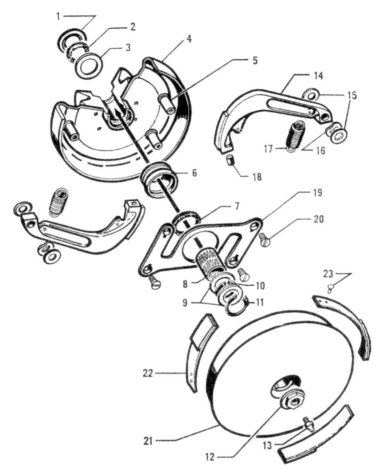

Fig. 25. Exploded View of Automatic Clutch and
Variable Pulley Fitted to Models RM.4, RM.6
and RM.8

1. Dished washer	13. Grease nipple
2. Felt seal	14. Clutch shoe
3. Plain washer	15. Plain washer
4. Clutch hub	16. Spring washer
5. Fulcrum pin	17. Clutch shoe return-spring
6. Retaining sleeve	18. Clutch shoe rubber stop
7. Felt seal	19. Retaining plate
8. Needle-roller bearing	20. Countersunk screw
9. Locating washer	21. Clutch drum
10. External circlip	22. Leaf spring
11. Internal circlip	23. Leaf spring rivet
12. Clutch drum nut	

Dismantling and Re-assembling Clutch Unit (Models RM.4, RM.6 and RM.8. It is assumed that the clutch drum and body have been removed as just described. The shoe retaining plate can now be detached from the unit (*see* Fig. 25) by removing the four countersunk screws holding it. These screws are actually locked in position but can be readily removed with a screwdriver of the correct size.

Remove the plain and spring washers on the clutch-pivot shoes and lift off the shoes. Then detach the shoe springs.

If it is necessary to replace the felt seal on the pulley side of the clutch the tabs holding the cap must be cut away before the cap and seal can be lifted out. A new seal can then be fitted in the cap, repositioned in the clutch hub and finally locked in position by punching over the rim of the recess.

When reassembling the clutch unit it is particularly important to note the correct position of the plain and spring washers on the shoe pivots. The four pivot pins are spaced irregularly and one plain washer should be placed over each pivot which is clockwise, i.e. to the right from its neighbour. Assemble the shoes and springs with the latter fitted in the holes which give the most tension. The shoes should be fitted over the pivots with the washers, so that the lining of each shoe is anti-clockwise, i.e. to the left from the pivot of the same shoe. One spring washer followed by one plain washer should then be fitted over the pivot, finally replacing the felt seal and the retaining plate. When the four countersunk screws are tightened down they should be locked by burring (with a punch) the end of the slot into the recesses in the flange.

Dismantling and Re-assembly Clutch Unit (Models RM.5, RM.9 and RM.12). In this case the automatic clutch (*see* Fig. 26) also includes the variable-gear unit. After the clutch drum and body base have been removed from the crankshaft, and the locating washer and needle-roller bearing lifted out of the hub, the clutch unit should be placed, shoes down, over the special clutch holding tool (*see* Fig. 27) mounted in a vice. The clutch centre fits over the central pin of the holding tool.

The fixed pulley check must now be removed. To do this, unscrew the 35 mm diameter centre nut which has a left-hand thread and then unscrew the pulley which has a right-hand thread, using a strap wrench if necessary. The pulley moving-cheek can then be lifted off followed by the plastic cage and the four steel balls.

Unscrew the four countersunk screws holding the clutch flange, using the correct size of screwdriver in order to break the lock and remove the flange. The shoes and springs can then be lifted out as a unit.

To re-assembly the clutch unit follow the reverse order of dismantling, noting that there is one plain and one curved washer on the pivot under each shoe. Also note that it is essential that the clutch shoes be fitted the right way round   The shoe springs are normally fitted in the holes neares the lining.

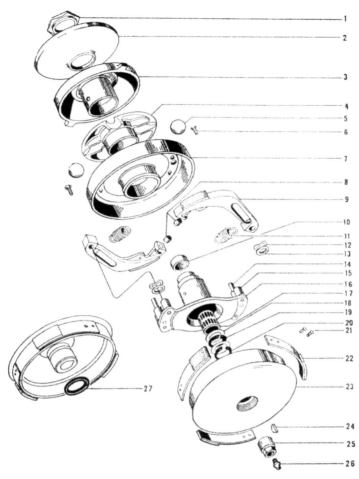

FIG. 26. EXPLODED VIEW OF AUTOMATIC CLUTCH AND
VARIABLE PULLEY FITTED TO MODELS RM.5, RM.9
AND RM.12

1. Fixed-flange pulley nut
2. Fixed-flange pulley
3. Sliding-flange pulley
4. Plastic cage
5. Steel ball
6. Countersunk screws
7. Clutch flange
8. Clutch shoe rubber-stop
9. Clutch shoe
10. Hollow plug for needle-bearing housing
11. Clutch shoe return-spring
12. Curved spring washer
13. Plain washer
14. Drive peg

15. Fulcrum pin
16. Clutch hub
17. Needle-roller bearing
18. Locating washer
19. External circlip
20. Internal circlip
21. Leaf-spring rivet
22. Leaf spring
23. Clutch drum with lined springs
24. Clutch drum key
25. Clutch drum nut
26. Grease nipple
27. Sealing ring

The flange should be refitted with the drive pegs through the centre pair of the six *outer* holes and the countersunk retaining screws should be burred into the flange recesses to lock them. Use new screws if the original screw-heads are at all damaged.

The steel balls should then be fitted into their plastic cage and the cage positioned with the balls *towards* the flange. The pulley moving cheek should then be placed in position with the *concave* side facing the flange. Finally screw on the pulley fixed cheek with the *convex* side towards the flange, using a strap wrench to tighten; secure by fitting and tightening the large diameter nut.

Refitting Clutch Unit. All parts should be thoroughly cleaned before refitting and the needle-roller bearing should be lightly greased. This

TABLE IX

SHIM WASHERS AVAILABLE FOR ADJUSTING CLUTCH END-FLOAT

Description		Thickness	Part No.
Shim washer for clutch hub	.	0·1 mm	MMW203
Shim washer for clutch hub	.	0·25 mm	MMW204
Shim washer for clutch hub	.	0·4 mm	MMW205

should be placed in position on the hub, followed by a thick locating washer, the smaller circlip, a second locating washer and then shim washer(s) of the correct thickness necessary to enable (*see* Table IX) the end flout (0·004 in.) of the clutch to be correctly adjusted. Finally refit the larger circlip, making sure that it is properly seated in its groove, centralize the smaller circlip relative to the washers and push the assembly onto the crankshaft until the smaller circlip locks into its groove on the shaft.

The clutch-drum key should then be located in the crankshaft slot, the use of a special clutch key positioning tool (*see* Fig. 27) being advisable for this. The projection on the key should face *away from the crankcase* in order to prevent the key from being dislodged when the clutch drum is fitted.

The clutch drum can now be refitted, together with its locking nut. On later models there is a plastic seal which must be correctly fitted on the groove in the centre boss of the drum.

The clutch body should have approximately 0·004 in. end float on the crankshaft. This end float is adjustable by inserting suitable shim washers behind the larger circlip, as already mentioned.

Should the clutch drum need relining, the heads of the rivets holding the leaf springs should be filed off and the rivets tapped out. New leaf springs can then be fitted with new rivets, taking care that the springs are fitted in the same position as before. When working on the clutch drum care should be taken to support the drum properly so that it does not become distorted. After refitting the springs the rivet heads should be filed or machined level with the inside surface of the drum.

GENERAL ENGINE OVERHAUL

Cylinder Head and Cylinder Barrel Removal. With the engine removed from the frame (*see* page 49), the clutch and flywheel magneto-generator should also be removed and the stator-plate mounting studs unscrewed. The cylinder head can then be removed and the cylinder barrel afterwards lifted off, taking care not to strain the four studs. The opening in the crankcase should be plugged with a clean cloth. This will prevent dirt or any objects entering the crankcase and it will also provide support for the easily damaged piston.

The piston rings can now be removed. Care must be taken when removing (and fitting) piston rings and they should not be sprung out wider than necessary.

Removing the Piston. The gudgeon-pin is shrunk fit in the piston and should only be removed if absolutely necessary. Removal of the gudgeon-pin circlips does not permit the gudgeon-pin to be pressed or driven out. It is necessary to warm the piston to approximately 250°F, and press out the gudgeon-pin with a special tool (*see* Fig. 27). Any other method of removal will almost certainly result in damage either to the piston or the small-end needle-roller bearing.

Renewing a Piston. Very close tolerances are employed on all Raleigh moped engines, and new pistons and cylinder barrels are normally available only as *matched* sets. If a new piston only is required, it is usually necessary on an earlier engine to return the cylinder barrel to enable the factory to exactly match a piston with it; on later models this is unnecessary, the matching piston being identified by the letter stamped on the top face of the cylinder barrel. Piston sizes (16) range from the size stamped "AA" (the smallest) to the size stamped "P" (the largest).

Fitting the Piston. This demands particular care. The small-end needle-roller bearing should be cleaned and oiled and placed in position in the connecting-rod eye. Then position the piston; make sure that it is right way round (the square cut-away in the skirt must face to the *rear*),* and temporarily mount it in position by inserting the long pilot drift of the gudgeon-pin extractor (*see* Fig. 27) through the small-end bearing and the piston bosses. The piston should then be warmed (to approximately 350°F) and the gudgeon-pin pressed in place with the special tool. At the

---

* The engines of Models RM.5 and RM.12 have a piston different to that fitted to Models RM.4, RM.6 and RM.9. On *all* engines the *piston ring pegs must face the exhaust port* when the piston is re-assembled. Therefore in the case of Model RM.5 and RM.12 engines the cut-away on the piston skirt must face the exhaust port or *front* of the engine.

same time this forces out the drift acting as the temporary gudgeon-pin for alignment purposes. Finally fit *new* circlips in the piston bosses, making sure that they are properly located in the grooves.

The Piston Rings. Only two sizes of piston rings are supplied as spares, namely 39·0 mm and 39·1 mm diameter. The smaller (39·0 mm) rings should be fitted to all engines marked from "AA" to "J"; and the larger (39·1 mm diameter) rings to engines marked "K" to "P".

Piston ring gaps on all engines must be set to between 0·004 in. and 0·008 in. when re-assembling. To check the gap of a ring place the ring in the cylinder bore, making sure that it is absolutely "square," and with the piston push it half an inch or so down the bore. Then check the gap with a feeler gauge. If it is too small, the gap can be enlarged by very carefully filing down the ends of the ring. If it is too large, a larger (39·1 mm) ring must be used with the gap adjusted, if necessary, as described above. Both piston rings should have their gaps checked in this manner. The side clearance of the pistons in their grooves should be practically nil.

Replacing Cylinder Barrel and Cylinder Head. When replacing the cylinder barrel a new gasket should be fitted at its base; also fit a new cylinder head gasket. Check that the piston rings are positioned correctly, lightly oil the cylinder barrel bore and slide the barrel into position over the piston rings. If difficulty is experienced in closing up the latter sufficiently to enable them to slip into the cylinder bore, a piston ring clamp (*see* Fig. 27) should be used.

With the cylinder barrel in position, check that the piston does not protrude above the top face of the cylinder barrel when in the T.D.C. position. If necessary, shims (*see* Table X) can be inserted under the base of the cylinder barrel to adjust the cylinder height.

Finally replace the cylinder head, checking that the gasket is positioned so that the hole for the decompressor outlets is in line with the hole in the cylinder barrel. Tighten the cylinder head nuts evenly, a little at a time and in a diagonal order.

Removing Main Bearings from Crankcase. To dismantle the crankcase, the cylinder barrel should first be removed (*see* page 59). The seven bolts holding the crankcase halves together can then be removed, together with the engine-mounting plates. Note that the crankcase bolts are not all the same; those which are threaded into the *top* of the crankcase have a coarser thread.

In order to free the main bearings from the crankcase a special tool (*see* Fig. 27) must be used and it is necessary to heat the crankcase to about 250°F with a flame, taking care to apply the heat evenly. The crankcase halves can then be separated by tapping the assembly on a wooden bench. The crankcase oil seals can be regarded as damaged by this operation and must be renewed when reassembling the crankcase.

TABLE X

SHIMS AND SHIM WASHERS AVAILABLE FOR ADJUSTING HEIGHT
OF CYLINDER BARREL AND THE CRANKSHAFT END-FLOAT

Description	Thickness	Part No.
Shim for cylinder barrel . .	0·2 mm	MTA145
Shim for cylinder barrel . .	0·4 mm	MTA146
Shim washer for crankshaft. .	0·1 mm	MMW168
Shim washer for crankshaft. .	0·2 mm	MMW169
Shim washer for crankshaft. .	0·3 mm	MMW170
Shim washer for crankshaft. .	0·75 mm	MMW177

Crankshaft End Float. If a *new* crankshaft is to be fitted its end float must be checked and adjusted as necessary. A used unit can be reassembled with the same shim washers as previously fitted between the main bearings and crankshaft webs, and with the shim washers in the same position as before.

When fitting a *new* crankshaft it is most convenient to use a pair of dummy bearings or a sliding-fit sleeve the exact width of the actual bearings (obtainable as spare parts). The crankshaft should then be mounted in the crankcase with these dummy bearings and shim washers (*see* Table X) fitted between the crankshaft webs and bearings until the correct end float (0·004 in.) is obtained. The maximum permissible end float is 0·008 in. Note that when selecting shim washers due allowance must be made for the thickness of the crankcase gasket; also the shim washers should be distributed as evenly as possible on each side of the crankcase webs.

Assembling the Crankcase Main Bearings. The main bearings are re-assembled by being driven onto each end of the crankshaft. A piece of metal $\frac{6}{16}$ in. thick should be placed between the crank webs to act as a support when the web can be rested on a vice and the main bearings driven onto each end of the crankshaft in turn, using a $\frac{5}{8}$ in. inside-diameter tube as a driver. This tube should bear only against the *inner* ring of the bearing.

Check that each bearing is fitted the correct way round, i.e. with the *larger* diameter towards the crank web.

Assembling Crankcase Halves. Fit *new* oil seals to the crankshaft, with the lips of the seals facing *outwards* (away from the crank webs). Warm one crankcase half and then slide it in place. Fit the gasket in position, warm up the other crankcase half and position it. Tighten evenly, but not excessively, (and with the engine-mounting plates in position), the bolts which secure the crankcase halves together.

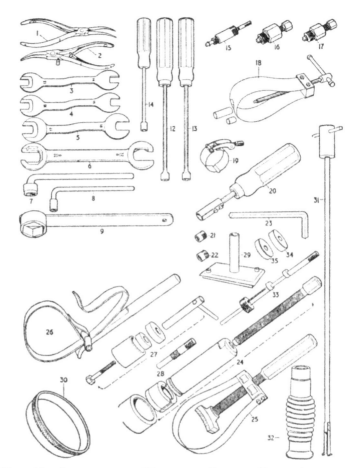

FIG. 27. SHOWING THE NUMEROUS SPECIAL TOOLS AVAILABLE
FOR POWER UNIT AND TRANSMISSION OVERHAUL

1. Circlip pliers (internal type)
2. Circlip pliers (external type)
3. Cone spanner (13 × 14 mm A.F.)
4. Cone spanner (15 × 16 mm A.F.)
5. Cone spanner (17 mm × 18 mm A.F.)
6. Steering head double-ended lock-nut spanner
7. Clutch drum wrench (14 mm A.F.)
8. Cylinder-head nut wrench (10 mm A.F.)
9. Clutch-hub nut wrench (35 mm A.F.)
12. Jet-socket spanner (9 mm A.F.)
13. Jet-socket spanner (8 mm A.F.)
14. Grease-nipple socket spanner (6 mm A.F.)
15. Ignition advance gauge
16. Magneto cam extractor
17. Clutch drum extractor
18. Gudgeon-pin extractor
19. Piston ring clamp
20. Clutch-key positioning tool
21. Thread protector (10 mm or 11 mm R.H.)
22. Thread protector (10 mm or 11 mm L.H.)
23. Flywheel-nut wrench (10 mm square)
24. Crankshaft bearing extractor
25. Flywheel holding tool (steel-band type)
26. Flywheel holding tool (webbing-strap type)
27. Engine-mounting rubber-bush fitting tool
28. Piston stop
29. Clutch holding tool
30. Coil centralizing ring
31. Front fork bush-removal tool
32. Magnetic extractor for clutch washers
33. Crankshaft/crankcase gauge
34. Dummy bearings (42 × 15 × 13 mm)
35. Dummy bearings (42 × 16 × 13 mm)

TOOLS FOR MAINTENANCE AND OVERHAUL

The Moped Tool Kit. The following nine items are supplied for general maintenance purposes in the standard tool kit issued with each new model—

Tyre pump and connector.

Spanner ($\frac{1}{8}$ in. $\times$ $\frac{3}{16}$ in. $\times$ $\frac{1}{4}$ in. B.S.F.).

Spanner (8 mm $\times$ 10 mm).

Spanner (12 mm $\times$ 14 mm).

Spanner for sparking plug and (1965-6 type) wheel spindle nuts.

Spanner for cylinder-head nuts.

Ring spanner (16 mm $\times$ $\frac{1}{2}$ in. B.S.F.).

Combination spanner.

Tommy-bar.

Special Tools Available. No less than 38 special tools are available as extras for comprehensive maintenance and overhaul of the power unit, transmission, etc. All of these tools except three are illustrated in Fig. 27 and can be readily identified by reference to the accompanying Key. Note that the abbreviation A.F. means "across flats" and that the tool numbers given are in no way related to the Part Nos.

7 Transmission overhaul

VEE-belt and drive-chain adjustment has been dealt with on pages 30 and 31 respectively in Chapter 3. Should some transmission overhaul become necessary, observe the following instructions, referring to Fig. 28 or 29 according to the type of moped you own.

Chain and Belt Removal. Detach both fairings so that the two chains can be removed (*see* page 30) and slacken the engine-mounting bolts to remove the primary drive Vee-belt (*see* page 30). In the case of Model RM.5 it is also necessary to remove the clutch guard and outer chain case to obtain access to the drive chains. On Model RM.12 the clutch guard only has to be removed.

To Remove Crank Axle with Pulley Assembly, etc. Remove the off-side crank cotter-pin and take off the crank, together with the chain-wheel. It will be found that a circlip and washer remain on the off-side of the axle. If these are removed the crank axle may be pulled out from its bearing from the near-side, together with the pulley assembly and sprocket. Note the position and size of any shim washers as these must be replaced in their original positions to maintain the required amount of end float (0·004 in.).

The Axle Bearing. The crank axle is carried in a plain bearing which is a press-fit in the frame. If it is necessary to replace this bearing it must be forced out and a new bearing press-fitted and subsequently reamed out to the required internal diameter (16 mm). It is unlikely that this bearing will become badly worn, however, unless it is damaged by water and grit thrown up by the wheels. To guard against this, enough grease should be injected to pass the thrust washer located between the pulley and the frame, when the pulley roller-bearings are lubricated.

Removing Pulley Assembly from Axle. To complete the dismantling of the bottom-bracket pulley the near-side cotter-pin and crank should be removed and the distance-piece slid off the axle. Remove the cap which is lightly pressed onto the pulley hub. The circlip can then be removed and the complete pulley assembly withdrawn from the axle.

The Drive Locking-lever. The drive sprocket runs freely on the pulley hub and is retained in position by a large washer on the axle between the frame and the pulley. A locking lever (shown at *A* in Fig. 30) is used to transmit the drive from the pulley to the sprocket and is operated by a turn-button on the outside of the pulley. This locking lever can be removed by unscrewing the nut on the outside of the pulley, removing the bolt and prising the spring off the peg on the turn-button as indicated in Fig. 30.

To refit the drive locking-lever, thread the spring and guide plate through the bracket on the pulley and locate the eye of the spring, and the guide

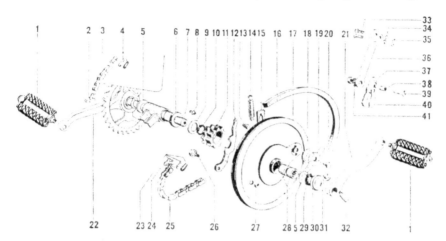

FIG. 28. TRANSMISSION DETAILS (MODELS RM.4, RM.6, RM.8 AND RM.9)

1. Pedals
2. Cranked link on pedal chain
3. Pedal chain (93 pitches)
4. Spring-link on 3
5. Spacing washer
6. Bottom bracket bush
7. Bottom bracket axle
8. Grease nipple
9. Spacing washer
10. Inner circlip
11. 12-tooth sprocket
12. Locking lever assembly
13. Locking lever spring rivet
14. Locking lever spring
15. Locking lever spring guide plate
16. Primary drive Vee-belt
17. Pulley and sprocket assembly
18. Turn-button spring disc
19. Turn-button locking lever
20. Turn-button fulcrum rivet
21. Pedal crank

22. Pedal crank and chain-wheel
23. Drive chain spring-link
24. Drive chain cranked link
25. Drive chain (96 pitches)
26. Fulcrum bolt
27. Nut for 26
28. Needle-roller bearing
29. Outer circlip
30. Pulley hub end-cap
31. L.H. crank spacer
32. Cotter-pin
33. Pedal chain tensioner-locking screw
34. Spring washer for 33
35. Nut for 33
36. Pedal chain tensioner assembly
37. Chain tensioner wheel
38. Bush for 37
39. Tensioner wheel spindle
40. Guide for pedal chain
41. Shake-proof washer and nut for 39

plate, over the peg on the turn-button. Insert the bolt on which the lever pivots through the lever and pulley, and fit the nut. The bolt threads just outside the nut should be lightly punched to lock the nut in place.

The Pulley Bearings. The pulley runs on two needle-roller bearings which are press-fitted. Old bearings can be driven out and new ones pressed back in place. The correct way round to fit them is with the maker's number on the bearings showing at each side of the hub. If the original bearings are removed from the pulley they must be replaced with new ones; once these bearings have been removed they are *not* fit for further use.

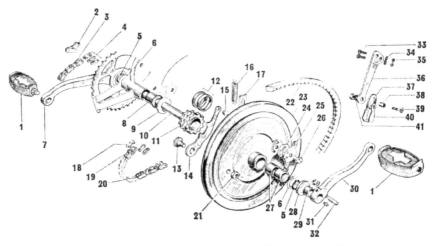

FIG. 29. DETAILS OF TRANSMISSION SYSTEM ON MODELS RM.5 AND RM.12

1. Pedals (solid rubber)
2. Cranked link of pedal chain
3. Pedal chain (93 pitches)
4. Connecting link of pedal chain
5. Circlip for bottom bracket axle
6. Spacing washer (16·5 × 26 × 0·5, 0·8 or 1 mm)
7. Chainwheel and R.H. crank
8. Bottom-bracket bush
9. Spacing washer (16·5 × 33 × 0·8 mm)
10. Bottom-bracket axle
11. Sprocket (11 teeth)
12. Plastic rings for bottom-bracket sprocket
13. Fulcrum bolt
14. Locking lever
15. Rivet pin for 14
16. Spring for 14
17. Guide plate for 16
18. Drive chain connecting link
19. Drive chain cranked link
20. Drive chain (95 pitches)
21. Nut for 13
22. Primary drive Vee-belt
23. Bottom-bracket pulley
24. Turn-button spring-disc
25. Turn-button locking lever
26. Turn-button fulcrum rivet
27. Needle-roller bearing for 23
28. End cap of pulley hub
29. Spacer for 30
30. L.H. crank
31. Bottom-bracket grease nipple
32. Cotter-pin
33. Chain tensioner securing screws
34. Spring washers for 33
35. Nuts for 33
36. Tensioner for pedal chain
37. Chain tensioner wheel
38. Chain tensioner bush
39. Spindle for 37
40. Pedal chain guide
41. Shake-proof washer and nut for 39

Re-assembling Pulley, Axle, etc. To refit the pulley and axle, insert the axle with the grease-nipple end on the near-side, and fit the shim washer and circlip on the off-side of the axle. On the near-side of the axle place the largest diameter washer adjacent to the frame, followed by the pulley, shim washer and circlip. Check that the crank axle end-float is approximately 0·004 in. If it is not, alternative sizes of shim washers (*see* Table XI) must be tried until the axle end-float *is* correct.

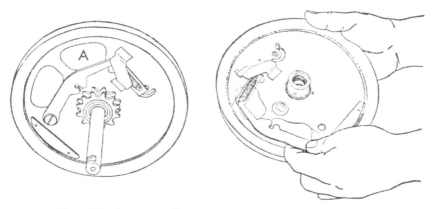

FIG. 30. SHOWING (AT A) THE LOCKING LEVER WHICH
TRANSMITS THE DRIVE FROM THE BELT PULLEY TO
THE CHAIN SPROCKET, AND (RIGHT) THE REMOVAL
OF THIS LEVER

In the right-hand sketch the locking-lever spring is shown being prised
off the peg on the turn-button.

TABLE XI

ALTERNATIVE SIZES OF SHIM WASHERS AVAILABLE FOR
ADJUSTING CRANKAXLE END-FLOAT

Description	Size	Thickness	Part No.
Shim washer .	27 × 16·5 mm	1·0 mm	MMW231
Shim washer .	27 × 16·5 mm	2·5 mm	MMW344
Shim washer .	27 × 16·5 mm	3·2 mm	MMW345
Shim washer .	27 × 16·5 mm	0·5 mm	MMW346
Shim washer .	27 × 16·5 mm	0·8 mm	MMW347
Shim washer .	27 × 16·5 mm	2·0 mm	MTD212
Shim washer .	33 × 16·5 mm	0·8 mm	MMW232
Shim washer .	37 × 16·5 mm	0·8 mm	MMW236
Shim washer .	33 × 16·5 mm	2·0 mm	MMW341
Shim washer .	33 × 16·5 mm	1·5 mm	MMW342
Shim washer .	33 × 16·5 mm	2·3 mm	MMW343

When correct axle end-float is obtained, refit the pulley hub cap,
tubular distance-piece and pedal cranks. Pull the engine backwards to
replace the Vee-belt and drive chains; then adjust the belt and chain
tension. Finally replace all transmission guards and fairings.

8 Controls and cables

THE handlebars, controls and control cables for the various Raleigh moped models are shown dismantled in Figs. 31–34 in this chapter, and the assembled layouts for specific models in Figs. 8–10 in Chapter 1. Although the handlebars and controls differ in minor details, their general design, operation and maintenance are basically the same for all models. The notes and maintenance instructions given in this chapter

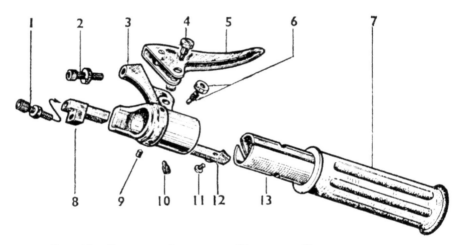

FIG. 31. COMBINED LAYOUT OF THROTTLE, DECOMPRESSOR AND FRONT BRAKE CONTROLS

The layout shown above applies only to Models RM.4 and RM.5 with a frame No. prior to H.1098.

1. Adjuster for decompressor cable
2. Adjuster for front brake cable
3. Twist-grip body
4. Pivot screw for 5
5. Lever for front brake cable
6. Retaining screw
7. Throttle twist-grip rubber

8. Decompressor cursor
9. Screw securing twist-grip body to handlebars
10. Retaining screw
11. Clamp screw for control cables
12. Throttle cursor
13. Twist-grip sleeve

therefore apply to *all* 1960–6 *models* unless otherwise stated. Reference should, of course, be made to the appropriate illustrations.

The Handlebar Twist-grip. The body of the twist-grip is secured to the off-side end of the handlebars by two or three screws, depending on the moped model concerned. With a three-screw fixing (used on Model

RM.5) the *largest* of the three screws has a reduced diameter portion which locates in the handlebars to ensure correct location. When refitting the twist-grip body this screw should be replaced first.

On *earlier* models the twist-grip sleeve carrying the rubber grip is attached to the main body by a retaining screw and a lock-nut located in front of the body. This sleeve can be detached by loosening the lock-nut,

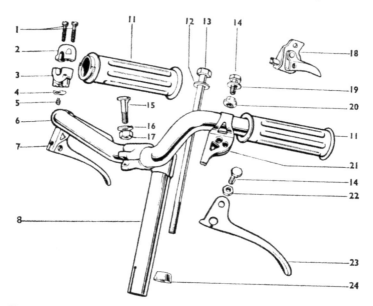

FIG. 32. EXPLODED VIEW OF HANDLEBAR ASSEMBLY (MODELS RM.4 AND RM.5)

1. Fixing screw for 2 and 3
2. Twist-grip body (top half)
3. Twist-grip body (bottom half)
4. Spring for twist-grip friction
5. Adjuster screw for 4
6. Handlebars
7. Fulcrum (front brake lever)
8. Handlebar stem
11. Plastic grips
12. Washer for 13
13. Expander bolt

14. Lever fulcrum bolt
15. Handlebar clamp bolt
16. Washer for 15
17. Nut for 15
18. Choke lever assembly
19. Plain washer
20. Fulcrum-clip nut
21. Fulcrum (rear brake)
22. Nut for lever fulcrum bolt 14
23. Rear brake lever
24. Expander cone

unscrewing the retaining screw and turning the grip in the direction (clockwise) used for closing the throttle. The sleeve, if removed, should be replaced in the reverse order of removal.

Both the throttle and decompressor cables are controlled by sliding cursors drawn along guides in the twist-grip body as the grip is rotated (*see* Fig. 31). A projection in the cursor engages with a spiral groove in the twist-grip sleeve, converting the rotary motion of the twist-grip into a "pull" action of the cable. Return action of both cables is automatically

obtained by a spring in the carburettor mixing-chamber for the throttle
and a spring attached to the decompressor plunger (*see* Figs. 17 and 18).

Twist-grip Friction Damping. The twist-grip rotary movement is
provided with friction damping on *earlier* models by virtue of the close
fit of the sleeve on the handlebars. If necessary, this damping can be

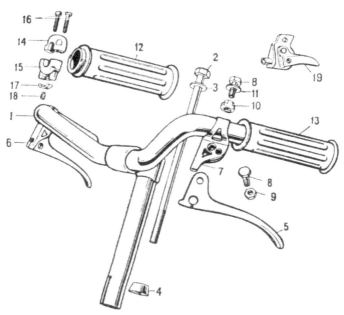

FIG. 33. EXPLODED VIEW OF HANDLEBAR ASSEMBLY
(MODELS RM.6, RM.8 AND RM.9)

1. Handlebars
2. Expander bolt
3. Washer for 2
4. Expander cone
5. Rear brake lever
6. Fulcrum (front brake lever)
7. Fulcrum (rear brake lever)
8. Lever fulcrum bolt
9. Nut for 8
10. Fulcrum-clip nut
11. Plain washer
12. Plastic grip (throttle twist-grip)
13. Plastic grip (near-side of handlebars)
14. Twist-grip body (top half)
15. Twist-grip body (bottom half)
16. Fixing screws for 14 and 15
17. Friction spring for twist-grip
18. Adjusting screw for 17
19. Choke lever

adjusted by removing the sleeve and squeezing it carefully in a vice, to
provide a tighter fit and more damping; or by increasing its internal diameter slightly by inserting a screwdriver or similar tool in the sleeve's
longitudinal slot and applying slight pressure to provide a looser fit and
less damping.

On all *later* moped models the twist-grip friction damping is provided
by a spring in the lower half of the twist-grip body and a small adjusting

screw (*see* Figs. 32–34) to vary the amount of damping. The screw should be adjusted so that the twist-grip will just stop in any position to which it is turned and released.

The Throttle and Decompressor Cables. The throttle and decompressor cables are operated by the cable nipples engaging slots in a cable-operating

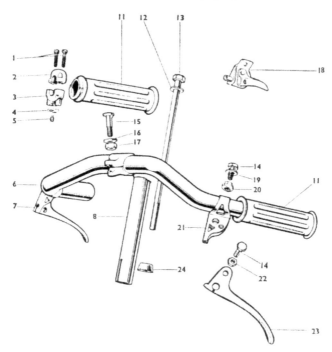

FIG. 34. EXPLODED VIEW OF HANDLEBAR ASSEMBLY
(MODEL RM.12)

1. Fixing screws for 2 and 3
2. Twist-grip body (top half)
3. Twist-grip body (bottomhalf)
4. Friction spring for twist-grip
5. Adjusting screw for 4
6. Handlebar bend
7. Fulcrum (front brake lever)
8. Handlebar stem
11. Plastic handlebar grips
12. Washer for 13
13. Expander bolt

14. Lever fulcrum bolt
15. Handlebar clamp bolt
16. Washer for 15
17. Nut for 15
18. Choke-lever assembly
19. Plain washer
20. Fulcrum-clip nut
21. Fulcrum (rear brake lever)
22. Nut for lever fulcrum bolt 14
23. Rear brake lever
24. Expander cone

drum. Removing the two screws (*see* Figs. 32–34) holding the twist-grip body to the handlebar end gives access to the cable-operating drum and the two cable nipples. To remove and fit the throttle and/or decompressor cable(s) the procedure required is as outlined in the following paragraphs.

Removing and Fitting Throttle Cable (Earlier Models). Remove the carburettor mixing-chamber cover and detach the throttle valve and spring. Then loosen the inner-cable clamp screw (located in the sliding cursor of the twist-grip) and withdraw the complete cable.

To replace a used cable, or fit a new one, place the cable in position on the machine and re-assemble the cable at the carburettor end first. The inner cable can then be inserted into the sliding cursor at the twist-grip end. Adjust the cable as necessary for proper operation and then tighten

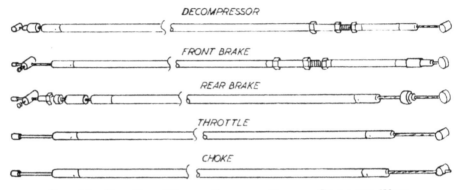

FIG. 35. THE FIVE MOPED CONTROL CABLES, COMPLETE WITH ADJUSTERS AND SOLDERLESS NIPPLES

The cables shown are fitted to all 1960 and subsequent models and each cable can be readily identified by reference to the above illustration

the inner-cable clamp screw in the sliding cursor. Finally adjust the throttle-cable adjuster shown at 8 and 11 in Figs. 17 and 18 respectively.

To Remove and Fit Decompressor Cable (Earlier Models). Detach the decompressor cable from the decompressor valve (a plunger) on the cylinder head (*see* page 51). Then loosen the inner-cable clamp screw in the twist-grip body, pull out the inner cable and remove the cable complete.

To fit a used or new decompressor cable (*see* Fig. 34), insert one end of the inner cable, with casing in position, through the twist-grip sliding cursor and into the twist-grip body. Re-connect the other end of the cable to the decompressor valve on the cylinder head and adjust the cable as necessary. Afterwards tighten the inner-cable clamp screw in the twist-grip body. Finally adjust the decompressor adjuster (*see* Fig. 8).

To Remove and Fit Throttle and Decompressor Cable (All Later Models). Remove the two screws holding the twist-grip body to the handlebars and lift off the top half. The appropriate cable nipple can now be released from the cable-operating drum. Detach the other end of the cable from the carburettor throttle-valve or the cylinder head decompressor-valve, according to which cable is being dealt with, and remove the cable complete.

To refit a throttle or decompressor cable (*see* Fig. 35), attach the cable at the joining face of the twist-grip body and push the lower half of the body into position on the cable-operating drum, when the nipple should spring into engagement with the drum. The twist-grip itself can then be re-fitted and the other end of the cable attached to the appropriate valve (throttle or decompressor).

If both the throttle and decompressor cables are replaced at the same time, be sure to position them the right way round at the handlebar end. The *throttle* cable should be in the *front* position and the decompressor cable at the rear. Adjustment of the throttle cable can be made at the carburettor mixing-chamber end (*see* page 45), and cable adjustment for the decompressor at the handlebar end as shown in Fig. 10.

Renewing the Choke Cable. The choke cable runs from a separate small control lever on the near-side of the handlebars (*see* Figs. 32–34). To replace this cable remove the carburettor mixing-chamber cover (*see* page 45) and detach the choke (enrichment) plunger and cable, drawing the cable through the slot in the cover. The clamp bolt on the choke lever can then be slackened and the inner cable pulled out from the lower end, together with the plunger and spring. These should be removed and replaced on a new cable (*see* Fig. 33) in the same manner.

To fit a new inner cable, insert it through the outer casing, reconnect its lower end to the choke plunger (with spring also), attach the lower end of the casing to the mixing-chamber cover and replace the cover on the mixing chamber. The upper end of the cable must then be secured by the clamp bolt, leaving about $\frac{1}{16}$ in. free movement in the cable with the choke lever in the *closed* position.

Renewing Brake Cables. Brake control cables can be removed for renewal, if necessary, simply by disconnecting the solderless nipples from each end (or one end) and pulling out the complete inner cable. A new inner cable (*see* Fig. 35) can then be fitted in its place and a solderless nipple added. Screw-type adjusters for front and rear brake cables are fitted at the handlebar lever pivots.

To Remove Speedometer-drive Cable (Models RM.5 and RM.12). The speedometer has a flexible drive-cable which must be disconnected at both ends. To detach the upper end, remove the headlamp rim, lens and reflector assembly and unscrew the upper end of the drive cable from the speedometer head. The lower end of the drive cable can be deteached from its drive unit by unscrewing the knurled collar.

In order to pass the lower end of the drive cable through the elongated hole in the fork leg (Model RM.5 only) it is necessary first to detach the cable ferrule after loosening the clip.

9 Wheels and front forks

THE front and/or rear wheel must be removed if the brake shoes or hub bearings require attention. This is seldom necessary. Routine bearing lubrication is dealt with in Chapter 1, and on pages 33–34 instructions are given for front and rear wheel removal.

THE FRONT WHEEL

It is assumed that the front wheel has been removed. Unscrewing the nut on the brake drum side and removal of the keyed washer enables the brake plate to be pulled off the wheel spindle. In the case of Model RM.5 with "swinging arm" type front forks the wheel spindle and speedometer-drive unit can be removed together. The wheel hub can then be dealt with as necessary. Make full use of the detailed front hub assembly drawings (Figs. 36–39) included in this chapter.

The Brake Shoes (All Models Except RM.6). To remove the brake shoes, it is only necessary to detach the cam lever and pull the brake shoe assembly away from the brake back-plate (*see* Figs. 36–38). The linings are bonded to the shoes and if badly worn, exchange-replacement lined shoes are called for. To fit brake shoes, assemble the shoes and return spring, place in position relative to the cam, align the shoe-pivot holes and fit onto the brake back-plate. Then re-assemble the cam lever in its correct position and fit and tighten the cam-lever nut. Finally fit the brake back-plate unit on the hub.

The Brake Blocks (Model RM.6). In the case of Model RM.6 the front wheel is of the normal bicycle type with external brake blocks actuating on the wheel rim instead of internal brake shoes inside the wheel hub actuating a drum. The brake blocks are, of course, very accessible for examination and renewal. Three important points to observe are: (*a*) when renewing brake blocks fit them the correct way round; (*b*) make sure that the blocks contact the wheel rim squarely; (*c*) oil the pivot pins on the calipers regularly.

Bearing Adjustment. The front wheel bearings (*see* Figs. 34–37) are of the cup-and-cone ball type, and are adjustable for wear (but not on Model RM.5 which has non-adjustable ball bearings). To make a bearing adjustment, first take off the near-side spindle nut and washer, and also the speedometer-drive unit (or spacer). Slacken off the near-side cone nut

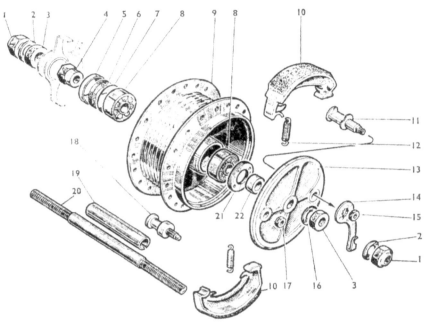

FIG. 36. THE FRONT HUB ASSEMBLY (MODEL RM.5 WITH "SWINGING ARM" TYPE FRONT FORKS)

1. Wheel spindle nut
2. Plain washer
3. Lock-nut, brake plate and speedo-meter-drive unit
4. Shouldered nut
5. Cap for 6
6. Felt seal
7. Plain washer
8. Ball journal-bearing
9. Front hub
10. Brake shoe
11. Brake cam

12. Brake shoe return-spring
13. Brake plate
14. Lever for 11
15. Nut for 11
16. Brake plate washer
17. Nut for 18
18. Pivot pin
19. Distance tube
20. Wheel spindle
21. Bearing retainer (L.H. thread)
22. Brake plate distance piece

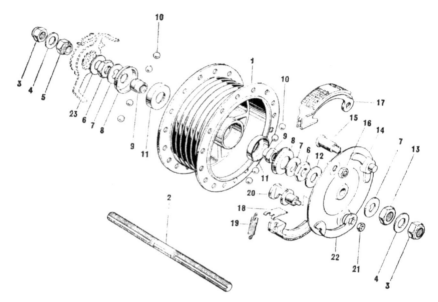

FIG. 37. THE FRONT HUB ASSEMBLY (MODELS RM.5 AND
RM.12 WITH TELESCOPIC TYPE FRONT FORKS)

1. Front hub
2. Wheel spindle
3. Nut for 2
4. Plain washer
5. Shouldered nut
6. Lock-nut for bearing cone
7. Keyed washer
8. Wheel bearing dust cap
9. Wheel bearing cone
10. Bearing balls
11. Wheel bearing cup
12. Brake plate spacing washer
13. Brake plate lock-nut
14. Brake plate
15. Pivot pin for 17
16. Nut for 15
17. Brake shoe
18. Brake shoe end-plate
19. Brake shoe return-spring
20. Brake cam
21. Nut for 20
22. Lever actuating 20
23. Speedometer drive-unit spacer

and pull the keyed washer behind the nut away from the cone. Screw the near-side cone in or out as required for adjustment and then tighten the lock-nut again with the washer in position. Bearing adjustment is correct when there is just *very slight play at the wheel rim* when the front wheel is fitted and the spindle nuts are firmly tightened.

Bearing Renewal. If the front wheel bearings need renewal, dismantle as previously described for bearing adjustment, but remove one cone

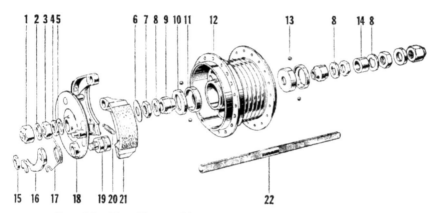

FIG. 38. THE FRONT HUB ASSEMBLY (MODELS RM.8 AND RM.9 WITH TELESCOPIC-TYPE FRONT FORKS)

This assembly applies to all Raleigh mopeds with telescopic-type front forks except Models RM.5 and RM.12.

1. Wheel spindle nut
2. Plain washer
3. Lock-nut
4. Keyed washer
5. Plain washer
6. Spacing washer
7. Cone lock-nut
8. Keyed washer
9. Bearing cone
10. Bearing dust caps (one for each bearing)
11. Bearing cup

12. Hub shell
13. Bearing balls (22 and of $\frac{7}{32}$ in. dia.)
14. Speedometer drive-unit spacer
15. Nut securing 16 to 19
16. Cam lever
17. Spring for 16
18. Brake back-plate
19. Brake cam
20. Brake shoe return-spring
21. Brake shoe
22. Wheel spindle

lock-nut completely and screw out the cone. Withdraw the wheel spindle from the opposite side and collect the steel balls which will fall out as the cones are removed. Prise off the dust covers on each side of the hub and tap out the bearing cups.

The hub should now be cleaned out completely of all old grease and new bearing cups fitted, taking care that these are assembled square with the hub. Repack the bearings with new grease of suitable type (*see* page 28). Then remove the old cone still on the wheel spindle and replace with a new one. New steel balls should now be fitted in the cups (10 on each side), and held in place with grease. Insert the wheel spindle and screw on the other cone. The cone positions should be adjusted so that there is 1⅝ in. of spindle protruding beyond the cone on the side opposite the brake drum. Replace the dust caps, keyed washers and cone lock-nuts, and adjust the bearings as described on page 74.

The same procedure as that just described is required for repacking the hub bearings with grease at 3,000 mile intervals as recommended on page 27, but the original parts can, of course, all be replaced except in the

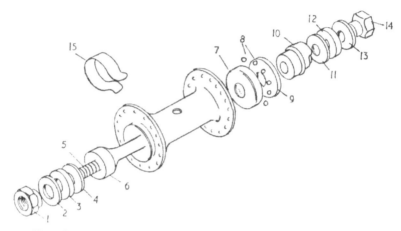

FIG. 39. DETAILS OF FRONT HUB ASSEMBLY (MODEL RM.6 WITH BICYCLE-TYPE FRONT FORKS)

The hub assembly also closely resembles a bicycle type.

1. Wheel spindle nut
2. Thin washer
3. Thick washer
4. Thin washer
5. Wheel spindle
6. Fixed cone
7. Bearing cup
8. Bearing balls (18 and of ¼ in. dia.)
9. Closure washer
10. Adjustable cone
11. Thin washer
12. Thick washer
13. Thin washer
14. Wheel spindle nut
15. Spring-cover for lubrication hole

unlikely event of any of them being appreciably worn. If any of the steel balls are damaged or worn, replace *all* of the balls, not just the faulty or suspected ones; old and new balls should *never* be assembled in the same wheel bearing.

THE REAR WHEEL

Once the rear wheel has been removed from the frame (*see* page 33) the brake plate is free to be withdrawn from the hub, full technical details of which are illustrated in Fig. 40.

The Brake Shoes (All Models). The brake shoes can be readily removed. Prise one of them away from the back-plate until it is disengaged from the cam and pivot, and then pull off both shoes, together with the return spring.

The brake linings, as in the case of the front brakes, are bonded to the shoes. Exchange-replacement lined shoes should therefore be fitted when the linings become badly worn. To fit the shoes, assemble the two shoes together, with their return spring attached, place one shoe in position

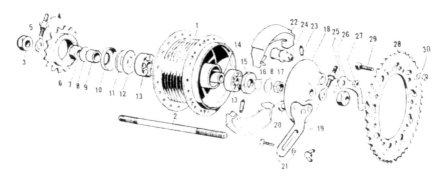

FIG. 40. EXPLODED VIEW OF REAR HUB AND SPROCKET ASSEMBLY

Basically its design is similar on all models.

1. Rear hub	17. Lock-nut
2. Wheel spindle	18. Brake plate
3. Nut for 2	19. Torque arm on 18
4. Chain adjuster assembly	20. Brake shoe pivot
5. Adjuster nut on 4	21. Screw, washer and wing nut on
6. Freewheel (18 teeth)	torque arm
7. Lock-nut	22. Brake shoe
8. Plain washer	23. Return spring for
9. Distance piece	24. Brake cam
10. Retainer for 11	25. Return spring for 24
11. Felt seal	26. Lever for 24
12. Hub bearing shield-washer	27. Nut for 24
13. Ball bearing	28. Rear wheel sprocket (54 teeth)
14. Bearing distance piece	29. Rear sprocket bolt
15. Bearing retainer	30. Nut and shake-proof washer for 29
16. Distance piece	

over the cam and pivot, and press down on the other shoe until it snaps into place.

Removing Hub Bearings for Renewal. The bearings of the rear-wheel hub have *non-adjustable* ball races and therefore if excessive play occurs due to wear, the bearings must be removed and *renewed*. The bearing on the brake-drum side is retained by a screwed plug with a right-hand thread and this bearing is intended to be removed with a special extractor (*see* Fig. 27). It can, however, be removed with a drift applied from the free-wheel side after the plug has been unscrewed. The bearing on the flywheel side can be readily removed, together with its felt seal, shim washer and cap.

To remove either bearing easily it may be necessary to dislodge the tubular distance-piece normally fitted between the bearings. Also when drifting out the bearing on the brake-drum side, take care not to damage the threads used for retaining the screwed plug. Note also *what* washers are included in the hub assembly (*see* Fig. 40) and *where* they must be positioned to ensure correct re-assembly.

Fitting New Ball Bearings. The bearing on the brake-drum side of the hub should be fitted first, followed by its screwed plug retainer. The wheel spindle can then be placed temporarily in position in order to slide the distance-piece in position, followed by a washer and the second bearing.

The felt seal and washers should now be placed adjacent to the bearing on the freewheel side, with the *flat* washer contacting the bearing. Then fit the distance-pieces or cap distance-pieces, as appropriate; referring to Fig. 40 as a guide. Finally fit the brake back-plate and replace the rear wheel in the frame.

THE FRONT FORKS

Four Types of Front Forks Fitted. The front forks fitted to 1960–6 Raleigh moped are of four types: (*a*) the "swinging arm" type fitted to the earlier Model RM.5 and shown dismantled in Fig. 43; (*b*) the earlier telescopic type shown dismantled in Fig. 41, fitted to the later Model RM.5 and the earlier version of Model RM.4; (*c*) the later and partially redesigned telescopic-type forks shown dismantled in Fig. 42, fitted to *all* later type mopeds except Model RM.6; and (*d*) the bicycle type forks fitted to Model RM.6 only.

Note that all Raleigh telescopic-type forks are of basically similar design. However, model RM.8, being a derivative of model RM.6 has these telescopic forks without covers. Model RM.6 itself has bicycle type (non-telescopic) forks. The dismantling and assembly instructions for telescopic-type front forks thus apply to all models RM.4, RM.5, RM.8, RM.11 and RM.12.

Fork Maintenance and Overhaul. The front forks require almost negligible maintenance except for occasional lubrication, and they rarely require major overhaul unless damaged in an accident. Should this become necessary, the best guide to correct dismantling and re-assembling of the forks is reference to an exploded view of the fork assembly concerned, namely Figs. 41, 42 or 43. The actual mechanical skill and work involved are quite straightforward and should be well within the capacity of the average moped owner.

Preliminary Dismantling for Fork Removal (Telescopic Type). The front wheel must, of course, be removed (*see* page 33), followed by removal of

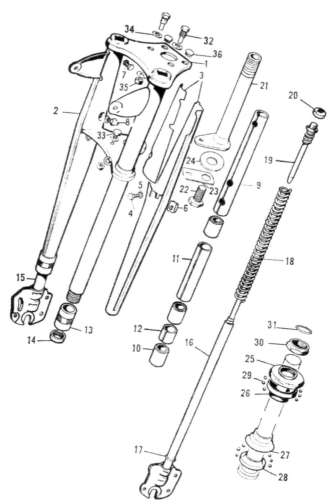

FIG. 41. FRONT FORKS OF THE TELESCOPIC TYPE
(EARLIER DESIGN)

1. Fork-tube assembly
2. Fork-tube cover (R.H.)
3. Fork-tube cover (L.H.)
4. Fork-cover bolt, 9 mm long
5. Shake-proof washer for 4
6. Fork-cover spacer
7. Fork-cover bolt (5·5 mm long)
8. Grease nipple
9. Upper spacer for fork tube
10. Fork-tube bush
11. Centre spacer for fork-tube
12. Lower spacer for fork-tube
13. Fork end-cap
14. Grease seal for 13
15. Telescopic leg
16. Telescopic leg
17. Stop ring on 15 and 16
18. Spring controlling fork action

19. Spring retaining rod
20. Slotted nut for 19
21. Steering stem
22. Bolt for 21
23. Locking plate for 22
24. Clamp washer
25. Adjustable bearing cone (steering head)
26. Upper ball bearing cup (steering head)
27. Lower ball bearing cup (steering head)
28. Lower ball bearing cone (steering head)
29. Bearing balls ($\frac{5}{16}$ in. dia.
30. Steering head lock-nut
31. Sealing ring for 30
32. Bolt (steering stop)
33. Bolt (locking plate)
34. Plain washer
35. Self-locking nut
36. Plastic plug (white)

the mudguard which is secured by three bolts at the bottom of each fork leg. The handlebars (*see* Figs. 32–34) must also be removed by loosening the expander bolt and tapping it to free the expander cone. The horn lead must also be disconnected and the horn removed from the fork plate.

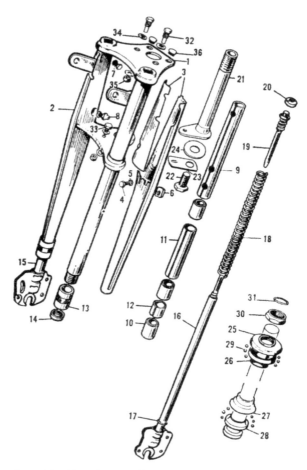

FIG. 42. THE LATER DESIGN OF TELESCOPIC-TYPE
FRONT FORKS

The design shown is fitted to all recent and current models. For key to
the numbered parts *see* page 81.

To Remove and Fit Telescopic Type-Front Forks. The large hexagon-headed bolt under the steering head should be removed, after flattening out the locking-tab, together with the steering head lock-nut. The forks can then be removed downwards by gently prising on the bottom plate and at the same time easing the forks forward away from the machine.

When the bottom plate is clear of the steering head the headlamp securing bolts can be removed and the lamp passed between the legs of the front forks. The forks can then be lifted off the steering stem.

The steering stem itself can be removed, if desired, by unscrewing the knurled adjustable race. This contains 25 steel bearing balls at each end of the stem; these should be carefully collected and counted.

To fit the telescopic-type front forks follow the reverse order of removal, noting that the two lugs entering the hole in the bottom plate must locate in the slots in the bottom of the steering stem. A new locking plate should be fitted under the large hexagon bolt, and the tab turned up to secure this bolt.

Dismantling and Assembling Telescopic-Type Front Forks. For dismantlingthe front forks completely, a special tool (*see* Fig. 27) is available so that all the bushes in one fork leg can be removed in *one* operation, together with the two lower spacing-tubes. However, the bushes, etc., can be removed *separately* without this tool, as they are a fairly slack fit. This job can be tackled with or without removing the front forks from the machine.

On Models RM.4, RM.9, RM.11 and RM.12 the front forks are fitted with covers. These covers are each secured by two bolts. To remove each cover the top bolt should be taken out, followed by loosening of the lower bolt. This detaches the inner cover and enables the outer cover to be slid down the leg of the fork. When re-assembling the front forks note that the fork covers are right- and left-handed. The forks themselves normally need no maintenance as they are sealed units, but are provided with a grease nipple on the inside at the top for periodic lubrication.

Dismantling "Swinging Arm"-Type Front Forks. In the case of the earlier version of Model RM.5 (introduced in 1960) the front suspension is of the leading, pivoted-fork type controlled by rubber bands (*see* Fig. 43). The fork itself is pivoted on bonded-rubber bushes which do not require any maintenance.

Early production models of the RM.5 moped were prone to suffer from displacement of the front suspension rubbers, which could result in some chafing of the front tyre. To cure this, retaining springs for the rubbers were subsequently fitted by the makers. On later RM.5 models (i.e. before the appearance of telescopic-type front forks) guide plates were welded to the lower bracket to act as front-suspension rubber retainers. Note that any earlier Model RM.5 not fitted with the above-mentioned guide plates can be fitted with retaining springs for the rubbers.

Dismantling procedure is different to that required for telescopic-type front forks. Start by removing the castle-nuts and their split-pins from the pivot bolts. After unhooking the rubber bands from the top anchorage, the pivot bolts can then be withdrawn and the fork removed.

Note that the rubber bands can only be removed from the forks by

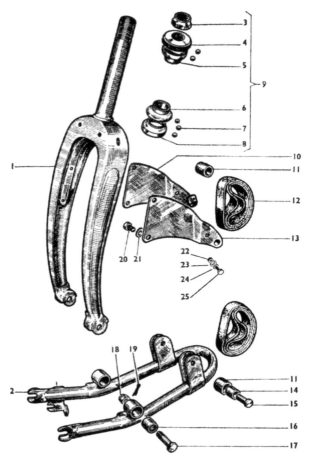

FIG. 43. FRONT FORKS PROVIDED WITH "SWINGING ARM"
(MODEL RM.5)

The later version of Model RM.5 has telescopic type front forks (*see* Fig. 42).

1. Forks
2. "Swinging arm"
3. Steering head lock-nut
4. Steering head cone
5. Upper bearing cup
6. Lower bearing cup
7. Bearing balls (50 and of $\frac{5}{32}$ in. dia.)
8. Lower bearing cone
9. Steering head-ball bearings
10. R.H. suspension plate
11. Rubber sleeve
12. Suspension rubber
13. L.H. suspension plate

14. Steel bush
15. Lower bracket rivet
16. Rubber pivot-bush
17. Pivot bolt
18. Castle nut for 17
19. Split pin
20. Bolt
21. Shake-proof washer for 20
22. Nut for 25
23. Shake-proof washer for 25
24. Plain washer for 25
25. Bolt

filing or grinding off the rivet heads and pushing out the rivets. The latter locate in a steel bush surrounded by a rubber sleeve.

Dismantling Bicycle-Type Front Forks. The front forks fitted to Model RM.6 can readily be removed complete, if necessary, from the end of the steering head.

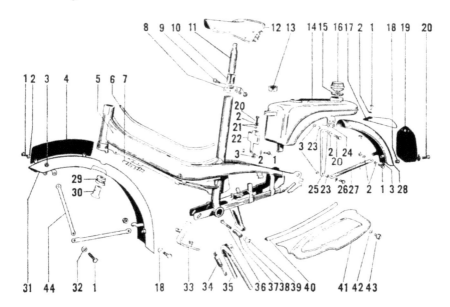

FIG. 44. FRAME, TANK AND MUDGUARD ASSEMBLY

1. Bolt, $\frac{3}{16}$ in. × $\frac{1}{2}$ in. dia.
2. Plain washer, $\frac{7}{16}$ in. dia.
3. Nut, $\frac{3}{16}$ in. dia.
4. Front number plate
5. Frame
6. Metallic trim strip
7. Bracket, cable retaining
8. Clip, saddle pillar
9. Bolt, complete, saddle pillar clip
10. Linear, seat tube
11. Saddle pillar
12. Saddle
13. Rubber mounting strip, fuel tank
14. Fuel tank
15. Sealing washer, filler cap
16. Fuel filler cap
17. Tailpiece
18. Spacer, $\frac{1}{8}$ in. thick
19. Rear number plate
20. Bolt, $\frac{3}{16}$ in. × $\frac{3}{4}$ in. dia.
21. Rubber washers, splash plate bolt
22. Splash plate
23. Spacer, $\frac{1}{4}$ in. thick
24. Pump peg
25. Tank support stay
26. Bolt, $\frac{3}{16}$ in. × $\frac{7}{8}$ in. dia.
27. Mudguard stay, pearl grey
28. Rear mudguard
29. Grommet, mudguard mounting
30. Tube, mudguard mounting
31. Front mudguard
32. Spring washer, $\frac{3}{16}$ in. dia.
33. Vee-belt guard
34. Spring, centre stand
35. Centre stand
36. Bolt, centre stand, complete
37. Distance piece, centre stand
38. Shakeproof washer, 7 mm dia.
39. Nut, 7 mm dia.
40. Plastic edging strip, L.H. 14 in.
41. Fairing, L.H.
42. Shakeproof washer, 5 mm dia.
43. Fairing screw
44. Mudguard stay

10 The "electrics"

"ELECTRICS" is a convenient abbreviation for a number of components and items which together constitute the partly combined ignition and lighting systems. They comprise: (*a*) the sparking plug; (*b*) the *external* H.T. ignition coil; (*c*) the flywheel magneto-generator; (*d*) the contact-breaker; (*e*) the electrical wiring; and (*f*) the lamps. For convenience these six items are dealt with in the above order which is not, of course, their order of functioning.

The Sparking Plug. To obtain maximum ignition efficiency always run with a recommended make and type of sparking plug fitted. The maker's recommendations are given under the heading IGNITION AND LIGHTING in the Specifications included in Chapter 1. Every 500 miles or so remove the plug and if necessary clean it and adjust its gap (in this order) as described on page 26.

The External Ignition Coil. This H.T. coil is mounted on the frame on all models and requires no maintenance other than keeping its terminals free from water, clean and tight. The coil is earthed by two mounting screws and if these are replaced or renewed it is most important to ensure good earth contact by first scraping clean and bright the areas of the frame which contact the two mounting bolts.

The Ignition Timing. In normal circumstances it is rarely necessary to check or adjust the ignition timing. The correct ignition timings for different engines are given adjacent to sparking plug recommendations in the Specifications included in Chapter 1 and also on page 54 where ignition timing procedure is fully dealt with.

THE FLYWHEEL MAGNETO-GENERATOR

All 1960–6 models are fitted with a "NOVI" flywheel magneto-generator which incorporates two coils, one for lighting and one for ignition, swept by the flywheel magnets. The basic electrical circuit is shown in Fig. 45.

An exploded view of the "NOVI" flywheel magneto-generator assembly (applicable to *all* models) is shown in Fig. 23 and is reasonably self-explanatory as regards the location and nature of the various components. The assembly is designed to give the minimum trouble and normally requires no maintenance other than paying routine attention to the contact-breaker. In the unlikely event of an ignition fault being caused by a faulty condenser or coil, either of these components can be readily renewed at little expense.

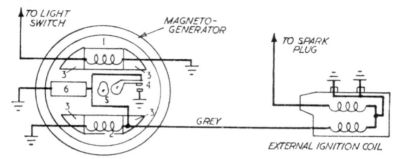

FIG. 45. THE BASIC ELECTRICAL CIRCUIT THROUGH THE MAGNETO-GENERATOR AND THE EXTERNAL IGNITION COIL

A wiring diagram showing the lighting and ignition circuits is shown in Fig. 46.

1. Lighting coil   4. Contacts of contact-breaker
2. Ignition coil   5. Cam
3. Pole pieces   6. Condenser

The Contact-breaker. The contact-breaker (*see* Fig. 24) is accessible after removing the flywheel from the crankshaft as described on page 51. Every 3,000 miles closely examine the contacts and if necessary clean them and adjust their gap (0·016 in.–0·018 in.) as described on page 53 in Chapter 6.

The Condenser. This unit is secured by two screws and washers and is connected to the contact-breaker insulated terminal by a lead. Removal and fitting of the unit is straightforward, but make sure that the above-mentioned lead is located well away from any moving parts.

The Ignition and Lighting Coils. These coils on the flywheel magneto-generator assembly are attached to the stator plate by a hollow screw and a hexagon screw with a slotted head. The ignition coil can if necessary be removed and renewed without disturbing the ignition timing. First disconnect the coil lead from the contact-breaker connexion and then remove the self-locking nut and the washers underneath. To remove the slotted hexagon-screw the tab on the washer must first be straightened. Finally remove the hollow screw and withdraw the ignition coil, preferably after removing the stator plate as described below.

The lighting coil has its output lead soldered to a terminal riveted to the stator plate. When the lighting coil is removed for renewal it is generally best to remove the stator plate (*see* Fig. 23) complete so that the output lead can be unsoldered from the terminal, or the terminal rivet drilled out. The stator plate is secured by two self-locking nuts to the coil pole-pieces, but before it can be pulled off its mounting studs the cam must be removed and the wires disconnected from the lighting terminal at the rear of the stator plate; the lead from the H.T. external ignition coil must also be disconnected. It is important when replacing the stator plate to make sure that the small sealing ring is in position on the crankshaft behind it.

If removal and renewal of one or both coils is necessary, a coil centralizing ring (*see* Fig. 27) should be used as described below to re-position the new coil(s) accurately. This is necessary to ensure that the coils have a constant minimum clearance between their pole-pieces and the flywheel, essential to obtain maximum electrical efficiency and output.

The ignition and lighting coils should first be assembled loosely on the stator plate and the centralizing ring then pushed over them to locate on four small tongues protruding from the threaded bosses on the stator. The coils can then be properly aligned by pressing against the inside of the centralizing ring, and afterwards firmly secured in this position. To remove the centralizing ring it may be necessary to turn it slightly while pulling it outwards.

THE LIGHTING CIRCUIT

A general wiring diagram of the lighting circuit is shown in Fig. 46. Current is supplied from the lighting coil on the flywheel magneto-generator to one side of the lighting switch, from which point is also taken

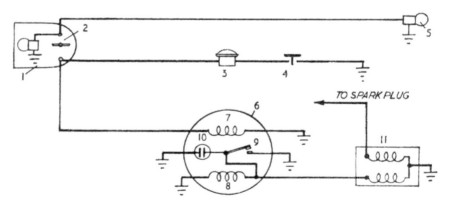

FIG. 46. GENERAL WIRING DIAGRAM SHOWING THE LIGHTING
AND IGNITION CIRCUITS

Note that the above diagram shows the *basic* arrangement of the two circuits and is not a fully comprehensive diagram issued by Raleigh Industries Limited or the makers of the electrical equipment. It applies to all 1960–66 Raleigh mopeds.

1. Headlamp
2. Headlamp lighting switch
3. Horn
4. Horn button
5. Tail lamp
6. Magneto-generator

7. Lighting coil
8. Ignition coil
9. Contact-breaker contacts
10. Condenser
11. External ignition coil

the lead to the electric horn. Another lead connected to the "ON" side of the lighting switch runs to the rear lamp. The horn thus operates on its own "power" circuit, while turning the lighting switch to the "ON" position connects the generator to the headlamp and the rear lamp.

Wiring circuits used differ slightly, according to the type of headlamp fitted. Earlier headlamps had a single "ON" position for the lighting switch, operated as described on page 17. On later rectangular-shaped headlamps the lighting switch has *two* "ON" positions, one for the normal driving beam, and the other for a dipped beam.

LAMPS AND BULBS

The Headlamp (Luxor and Wipac). The bulb on a Luxor headlamp is accessible for removal and renewal after removing the lamp rim and reflector assembly by pressing the bulb holder *towards* the reflector, turning it *anti-clockwise* and withdrawing it. The bulb on the Wipac headlamp (Models RM.8 and RM.9) has a staggered pin connection but removal and replacement is otherwise similar.

The *correct type bulbs* to fit on Luxor, Sturmey Archer or Wipac headlamps are specified in Table XII. Where the headlamp has a two-position lighting switch, care must be taken to fit the bulb the correct way round. For some headlamps (Luxor) the contact pins are of unequal length to prevent the bulb being fitted incorrectly. With other headlamps (Wipac) the pins are offset to ensure correct bulb fitting, and the reflector is dimpled to prevent incorrect fitting of the bulb holder. Focusing adjustment is not necessary or provided on any Lucas or Wipac headlamps fitted to Raleigh mopeds.

TABLE XII

CORRECT BULBS FOR FITTING TO 1960–6 HEADLAMPS AND
REAR LAMPS

Lamp	Make and Shape	Correct Bulb	Moped Model
Headlamp	Luxor (Rectangular)	6 V, 15 W, S.B.C.	RM.4, RM.5
Headlamp	Sturmey Archer	6 V, 15 W, S.C.C.	RM.6
Headlamp	Luxor (Round)	6 V, 15/15 W, S.C.C.	RM.11, RM.12
Headlamp	Wipac (Round)	6 V, 15/15 W, S.B.C.	RM.8, RM.9
Rear lamp	Lucas	6 V, 3 W, M.E.S.	—Miscellaneous
Rear lamp	Miller (Types A, B, C)	6 V, 3 W, S.C.C.	—*See* text
Rear lamp	Wipac	6 V, 3 W, M.E.S.	—Miscellaneous

Miller Rear Lamps. Three different types of Miller rear lamps have been fitted to 1960–6 Raleigh mopeds. The lamp first fitted has twice been modified in order to comply with existing lighting regulations. The three types can be identified by the following essential differences—

TYPE A

This rear lamp, fitted to earlier models, has a centrally-positioned bulb holder, a domed lens and cheese-headed mounting screws.

TYPE B

This lamp, fitted instead of type A to later models, has the same back-plate as type A but its lens is angular and its entire rear portion flat. The lens mounting-screws have countersunk heads and are longer than those used on the type A lamp. To ensure the maximum projection of red light to the rear, the centre of the lamp reflecting surface has a clear red circle positioned directly over the bulb.

TYPE C

The latest type of Miller rear lamp, fitted to many recent and all current Raleigh mopeds, is similar to the type B lamp, but the bulb holder and red circle in the lamp reflecting surface are located higher up.

Lenses and Bulbs for Miller Rear Lamps. Note that the lenses for type B and C rear lamps are *not* interchangeable and that those for types A and B *are* interchangeable. Spare lenses supplied are therefore those designed for type A and C rear lamps, the former being, of course, suitable for type B.

The bulb specified in Table XII is suitable for all three types of Miller rear lamps.

Lucas and Wipac Rear Lamps. On some mopeds a Lucas or Wipac rear lamp is fitted instead of one of the three above-mentioned Miller types. These are of straightforward modern design and their bulbs are readily accessible. Correct types of bulbs to fit are those specified in Table XII. Although the bulbs are of similar type for Lucas and Wipac lamps, it is advisable to fit bulbs of the appropriate make.

LIGHTING FAULTS

Faults which usually develop in the lighting system are most likely to be caused by a blown bulb, dirty or loose connexions or chafed or damaged wiring. If lamp bulbs persistently burn out, the following checks should be made—

1. Check that the lamp bulbs are properly mounted in their holders.
2. Inspect all connexions, especially *earth* connexions.
3. Check the condition and action of the headlamp lighting switch and, if necessary clean its contacts.
4. Examine all leads in the wiring system for chafing or damage.

Index

AUTOBOOKS WORKSHOP MANUALS

ALFA ROMEO GIULIA 1300, 1600, 1750, 2000 1962-1978 WSM
BMW 1600 1966-1973 WSM
BMW 2000 & 2002 1966-1976 WSM
BMW 2500, 2800, 3.0 & 3.3 1968-1977 WSM
BMW 316, 320, 320i 1975-1977 WSM
BMW 518, 520, 520i 1973-1981 WSM
FIAT 1100, 1100D, 1100R & 1200 1957-1969 WSM
FIAT 124 1966-1974 WSM
FIAT 124 SPORT 1966-1975 WSM
FIAT 125 & 125 SPECIAL 1967-1973 WSM
FIAT 126, 126L, 126 DV, 126/650 & 126/650 DV 1972-1982 WSM
FIAT 127 SALOON, SPECIAL & SPORT, 900, 1050 1971-1981 WSM
FIAT 128 1969-1982 WSM
FIAT 1300, 1500 1961-1967 WSM
FIAT 131 MIRAFIORI 1975-1982 WSM
FIAT 132 1972-1982 WSM
FIAT 500 1957-1973 WSM
FIAT 600, 600D & MULTIPLA 1955-1969 WSM
FIAT 850 1964-1972 WSM
JAGUAR E-TYPE 1961-1972 WSM
JAGUAR MK 1, 2 1955-1969 WSM
JAGUAR S TYPE, 420 1963-1968 WSM
JAGUAR XK 120, 140, 150 MK 7, 8, 9 1948-1961 WSM
LAND ROVER 1, 2 1948-1961 WSM
MERCEDES-BENZ 190 1959-1968 WSM
MERCEDES-BENZ 220/8 1968-1972 WSM
MERCEDES-BENZ 220B 1959-1965 WSM
MERCEDES-BENZ 230 1963-1968 WSM
MERCEDES-BENZ 250 1968-1972 WSM
MERCEDES-BENZ 280 1968-1972 WSM
MG MIDGET TA-TF 1936-1955 WSM
MINI 1959-1980 WSM
MORRIS MINOR 1952-1971 WSM
PEUGEOT 404 1960-1975 WSM
PORSCHE 911 1964-1973 WSM
PORSCHE 911 1970-1977 WSM
RENAULT 16 1965-1979 WSM
RENAULT 8, 10, 1100 1962-1971 WSM
ROVER 3500, 3500S 1968-1976 WSM
SUNBEAM RAPIER, ALPINE 1955-1965 WSM
TRIUMPH SPITFIRE, GT6, VITESSE 1962-1968 WSM
TRIUMPH TR2, TR3, TR3A 1952-1962 WSM
TRIUMPH TR4, TR4A 1961-1967 WSM
VOLKSWAGEN BEETLE 1968-1977 WSM

VELOCEPRESS AUTOMOBILE BOOKS & MANUALS

ABARTH BUYERS GUIDE
AUSTIN-HEALEY 6-CYLINDER WSM
AUSTIN-HEALEY SPRITE & MG MIDGET 1958-1971 WSM
BMW 600 LIMOUSINE FACTORY WSM
BMW 600 LIMOUSINE OWNERS HAND BOOK & SERVICE MANUAL
BMW ISETTA FACTORY WSM
BOOK OF THE CARRERA PANAMERICANA - MEXICAN ROAD RACE
COMPLETE CATALOG OF JAPANESE MOTOR VEHICLES
CORVAIR 1960-1969 OWNERS WORKSHOP MANUAL
CORVETTE V8 1955-1962 OWNERS WORKSHOP MANUAL
DIALED IN - THE JAN OPPERMAN STORY
FERRARI 250/GT SERVICE AND MAINTENANCE
FERRARI 308 SERIES BUYER'S AND OWNER'S GUIDE
FERRARI BERLINETTA LUSSO
FERRARI BROCHURES AND SALES LITERATURE 1946-1967
FERRARI BROCHURES AND SALES LITERATURE 1968-1989
FERRARI GUIDE TO PERFORMANCE
FERRARI OPP, MAINTENANCE & SERVICE H/BOOKS 1948-1963
FERRARI OWNER'S HANDBOOK
FERRARI SERIAL NUMBERS PART I - ODD NUMBERS TO 21399
FERRARI SERIAL NUMBERS PART II - EVEN NUMBERS TO 1050
FERRARI SPYDER CALIFORNIA
FERRARI TUNING TIPS & MAINTENANCE TECHNIQUES
HENRY'S FABULOUS MODEL "A" FORD
HOW TO BUILD A FIBERGLASS CAR
HOW TO BUILD A RACING CAR
HOW TO RESTORE THE MODEL 'A' FORD
IF HEMINGWAY HAD WRITTEN A RACING NOVEL
JAGUAR E-TYPE 3.8 & 4.2 WSM
LE MANS 24 (THE BOOK THAT THE FILM WAS BASED ON)
MASERATI BROCHURES AND SALES LITERATURE
MASERATI OWNER'S HANDBOOK
METROPOLITAN FACTORY WSM
MGA & MGB OWNERS HANDBOOK & WSM
OBERT'S FIAT GUIDE
PERFORMANCE TUNING THE SUNBEAM TIGER
PORSCHE 356 1948-1965 WSM
PORSCHE 912 WSM
SOUPING THE VOLKSWAGEN
TRIUMPH TR2, TR3, TR4 1953-1965 WSM
TUNING FOR SPEED (P.E. IRVING)
VEDA ORR'S NEW REVISED HOT ROD PICTORIAL
VOLKSWAGEN TRANSPORTER, TRUCKS, STATION WAGONS WSM
VOLVO 1944-1968 ALL MODELS WSM
WEBER CARBURETORS (EMPHASIS ON ALFA & FIAT)

BROOKLANDS BOOKS & ROAD TEST PORTFOLIOS (RTP)

AC CARS 1904-2009
ALFA ROMEO 1920-1933 ROAD TEST PORTFOLIO
ALFA ROMEO 1934-1940 ROAD TEST PORTFOLIO
BRABHAM RALT HONDA THE RON TAURANAC STORY
BUGATTI TYPE 10 TO TYPE 40 ROAD TEST PORTFOLIO
BUGATTI TYPE 10 TO TYPE 251 ROAD TEST PORTFOLIO
BUGATTI TYPE 41 TO TYPE 55 ROAD TEST PORTFOLIO
BUGATTI TYPE 57 TO TYPE 251 ROAD TEST PORTFOLIO
DELAHAYE ROAD TEST PORTFOLIO
FERRARI ROAD CARS 1946-1956 ROAD TEST PORTFOLIO
FIAT 500 1936-1972 ROAD TEST PORTFOLIO
FIAT DINO ROAD TEST PORTFOLIO
HISPANO SUIZA ROAD TEST PORTFOLIO
HONDA ST1100/ST1300 PAN EUROPEAN 1990-2002 RTP
JAGUAR MK1 & MK2 ROAD TEST PORTFOLIO
LOTUS CORTINA ROAD TEST PORTFOLIO
MV AGUSTA F4 750 & 1000 1997-2007 ROAD TEST PORTFOLIO
TATRA CARS ROAD TEST PORTFOLIO

VELOCEPRESS MOTORCYCLE BOOKS & MANUALS

AJS SINGLES & TWINS 250cc THRU 1000cc 1932-1948 (BOOK OF)
AJS SINGLES 1955-65 350cc & 500cc (BOOK OF)
AJS SINGLES 1945-60 350cc & 500cc MODELS 16 & 18 (BOOK OF)
ARIEL 1939-1960 4 STROKE SINGLES (BOOK OF)
ARIEL LEADER & ARROW 1958-1964 (BOOK OF)
ARIEL MOTORCYCLES 1933-1951 WSM
ARIEL PREWAR MODELS 1932-1939 (BOOK OF)
BMW M/CYCLES R26 R27 (1956-1967) FACTORY WSM
BMW M/CYCLES R50 R50S R60 R69S (1955-1969) FACTORY WSM
BSA BANTAM (BOOK OF)
BSA ALL FOUR-STROKE SINGLES & V-TWINS 1936-1952 (BOOK OF)
BSA OHV & SV SINGLES - 250cc 1954-1970 (BOOK OF)
BSA OHV & SV SINGLES 1945-54 250-600cc (BOOK OF)
BSA OHV SINGLES 350 & 500cc 1955-1967 (BOOK OF)
BSA PRE-WAR MODELS TO 1939 (BOOK OF)
BSA TWINS 1948-1962 (BOOK OF)
BSA TWINS 1962-1969 (SECOND BOOK OF)
CATALOG OF BRITISH MOTORCYCLES (1951 MODELS)
DOUGLAS PRE-WAR ALL MODELS 1929-1939 (BOOK OF)
DOUGLAS POST-WAR ALL MODELS 1948-1957 FACTORY WSM
DUCATI 160cc, 250cc & 350cc OHC MODELS FACTORY WSM
HONDA 50 ALL MODELS UP TO 1970 INC MONKEY & TRAIL (BOOK OF)
HONDA 90 ALL MODELS UP TO 1966 (BOOK OF)
HONDA MOTORCYCLES 125-150 TWINS C/CS/CB/CA WSM
HONDA MOTORCYCLES 250-305 TWINS C/CS/CB WSM
HONDA MOTORCYCLES C100 SUPER CUB WSM
HONDA MOTORCYCLES C110 SPORT CUB 1962-1969 WSM
HONDA TWINS & SINGLES 50cc THRU 305cc 1960-1966 (BOOK OF)
HONDA TWINS ALL MODELS 125cc THRU 450cc UP TO 1968 (BOOK OF)
INDIAN PONYBIKE, BOY RACER & PAPOOSE ILL PARTS LIST & SALES LIT
LAMBRETTA ALL 125 & 150cc MODELS 1947-1957 (BOOK OF)
LAMBRETTA LI & TV MODELS 1957-1970 (SECOND BOOK OF)
MATCHLESS 350 & 500cc SINGLES 1945-1956 (BOOK OF)
MATCHLESS 350 & 500cc SINGLES 1955-1966 (BOOK OF)
NORTON 1932-1947 (BOOK OF)
NORTON 1938-1956 (BOOK OF)
NORTON DOMINATOR TWINS 1955-1965 (BOOK OF)
NORTON MODELS 19, 50 & ES2 1955-1963 (BOOK OF)
NORTON MOTORCYCLES 1957-1970 FACTORY WSM
NORTON PREWAR MODELS 1932-1939 (BOOK OF)
NSU QUICKLY ALL MODELS 1953-1963 (BOOK OF)
RALEIGH MOPEDS 1960-1969 (BOOK OF)
ROYAL ENFIELD SINGLES & V TWINS 1937-1953 (BOOK OF)
ROYAL ENFIELD SINGLES 1946-1962 (BOOK OF)
ROYAL ENFIELD 736cc INTERCEPTOR FACTORY WSM
ROYAL ENFIELD 250cc & 350cc SINGLES 1958-1966 (SECOND BOOK OF)
SUNBEAM S7 & S8 (BOOK OF)
SUZUKI 50cc & 80cc UP TO 1966 (BOOK OF)
SUZUKI T10 1963-1967 FACTORY WSM
SUZUKI T20 & T200 1965-1969 FACTORY WSM
TRIUMPH PRE-WAR MOTORCYCLE 1935-1939 (BOOK OF)
TRIUMPH MOTORCYCLES 1937-1951 WSM
TRIUMPH MOTORCYCLES 1945-1955 FACTORY WSM
TRIUMPH TWINS 1956-1969 (BOOK OF)
VELOCETTE ALL SINGLES & TWINS 1925-1970 (BOOK OF)
VESPA 1951-1961 (BOOK OF)
VESPA 125 & 150cc & GS MODELS 1955-1963 (SECOND BOOK OF)
VESPA 90, 125 & 150cc 1963-1972 (THIRD BOOK OF)
VESPA GS & SS 1955-1968 (BOOK OF)
VILLIERS ENGINE (BOOK OF)
VINCENT MOTORCYCLES 1935-1955 WSM

PLEASE VISIT OUR WEBSITE
www.VelocePress.com
FOR A DETAILED DESCRIPTION
OF ANY OF THESE TITLES

Please check our website:

www.VelocePress.com

for a complete
up-to-date list of
available titles

Milton Keynes UK
Ingram Content Group UK Ltd.
UKHW021357060824
1175UKWH00040B/491